to be re

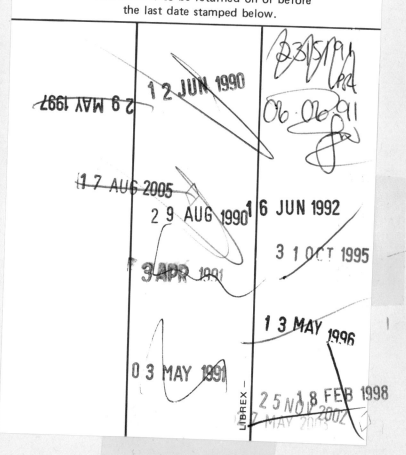

This book is to be returned on or before
the last date stamped below.

2 9 MAY 1997

1 2 JUN 1990

16.90.91

1 7 AUG 2005

2 9 AUG 1990 1 6 JUN 1992

3 1 OCT 1995

3 APR 1991

1 3 MAY 1996

0 3 MAY 1991

LIBREX —

2 5 NOV 18 FEB 1998

7 MAY 2002

MONOGRAPHS IN ELECTRICAL AND ELECTRONIC ENGINEERING

EDITORS: P. HAMMOND, D. WALSH

Low-noise electrical motors

S. J. YANG

Heriot-Watt University

CLARENDON PRESS · OXFORD
1981

Oxford University Press, Walton Street, Oxford OX2 6DP

London Glasgow New York Toronto
Delhi Bombay Calcutta Madras Karachi
Kuala Lumpur Singapore Hong Kong Tokyo
Nairobi Dar es Salaam Cape Town Salisbury
Melbourne Auckland

and associate companies in
Beirut Berlin Ibadan Mexico City

© S. J. Yang, 1981

Published in the United States by Oxford University Press, New York

British Library Cataloguing in Periodicals Data

Yang, S. J.
  Low-noise electrical motors. – (Monographs
  in electrical and electronic engineering)
  1. Electrical motors
  I. Title   II. Series
  621.46'2   TK2511

  ISBN 0-19-859332-5

Typeset by Alden Press, Finchley

Printed in Great Britain
at the University Press, Oxford
by Eric Buckley
Printer to the University

Foreword

Dr. Yang has produced a valuable and timely book. It will be of great assistance to all designers and manufacturers of electric machines, because noise and the need for its reduction is generally, even governmentally, recognised as of enormous importance in improving the quality of life. The result of this recognition has been the publication in many countries of noise standards and a growing tendency for the noise level produced by devices to figure in purchasers' specifications. It is now important for every manufacturer to produce rotating machines meeting given noise criteria in an optimum (cost effective) way. A clear understanding of how electric machines produce noise and how it is measured is essential. The need to know within given limits and at the design stage the noise spectrum which a machine will produce when built is therefore real and the means for reducing the noise if it is too high, involving a clear understanding of the physical characteristics and limitations of materials and structures, is important if the result is to be optimum.

The subject of electric machine noise was an art rather like cookery until relatively recent years. All induction motor designers, for example, had (and some still do) a list of 'forbidden combinations' of stator and rotor slots. Disappointments were not infrequent when a machine which 'should have' been quiet turned out noisy on test. Twenty or thirty years ago all that was perfectly clear appeared to be that quiet machines should have low flux densities in their magnetic parts, skewed slots, a very heavy structure, no fans and sleeve bearings. This was the situation when I left industry in 1958 and decided to try to do something about it. So we started a research team at Queen Mary College (University of London), designed and built a new-style anechoic chamber and began studies of the noise field around electric machines. We came a long way in the next 14 years and the author of this book, Dr. Yang, was a major contributor to the results of that splendid team. Our ultimate aim was to acquire, if possible, the means to predict, within known limits, the complete noise spectrum of an electric machine at the design stage. We learned how to measure noise; we acquired some understanding of how the various components of the spectrum were produced; and we moved a long way towards that goal. We learned first elementary things such as that the noise from a machine depends not only on the noise-causing forces (depending, inter alia, on slot numbers) but also on the response to those forces of the structure, and to the radiating characteristics of that structure. (A noisy machine often was the result not of just a 'forbidden' slot combination but more importantly of a condition of resonance between forcing frequencies and structure vibratory characteristics. The old style electrical design engineer was unable to calculate the natural frequencies of the mechanical structure.)

These were interesting days spanning electric power, energy conversion, mechanical vibrations, physics especially acoustics, electronics, and mathematics. Truly versatile engineers in the real sense of that term were stretched to their limits. Dr. Yang's book summarises some of the results of that work, and much of his own, carried out since. My wish is that it will be a great help to electric machine designers throughout the world. It is certainly needed on their shelves.

A. J. Ellison

Acknowledgements

I should like to thank Professor A.J. Ellison and Dr. C.J. Moore, who introduced me to the challenging and interesting problems of noise in electrical machines fourteen years ago at Queen Mary College, University of London. I could not have begun without their guidance and encouragement. I am also indebted to many friends in industry and academic institutions, both in the United Kingdom and overseas, for their many stimulating discussions.

Grateful thanks must go to Mr. R. Jensen for his constructive comments on the draft and to Mrs. S. Murray, Mrs. H. Vaughan, Mrs. F. Samson, Mrs. P. Ingram, Mrs. M. Crawford, for typing the manuscript.

I am indebted to the Institution of Electrical Engineers, London; the American Society of Mechanical Engineers, New York; B.B.C. Brown Boveri & Co., Baden; Academic Press Ltd., London; and S. Hirzel Verlag, Stuttgart for permission to use the material in many papers published by them.

Heriot-Watt University, Edinburgh,   *S.J. Yang*
January 1981.

To Mr. and Mrs. Y. M. Wong

Contents

1. Introduction

1.1. Introduction

In the *Glossary of Acoustic Terms* by the British Standards Institution (1955), noise is defined as sound which is undesired by the recipient.

Noise may interfere with speech and our ability to think, make sleep difficult and cause fatigue. Prolonged loud noise can damage hearing and cause pain, fainting and psychosis. Efforts have been made to assess the psychological and physiological effects of noise on human beings but our knowledge of these aspects is still not large. Nevertheless, fairly satisfactory methods have been developed to assess effects of a steady noise.

The life of everyone is, to a certain degree, bound up with various machines. They either help us get more from natural resources or make life easier and more efficient. However, they often produce unpleasant noise. As a result, our environment is becoming noisier. In order to ensure a reasonable environment for people to live and to work, various countries have set up laws to limit noise pollution. For example, in the USA, the Bureau of Labor Standards added a safety regulation on industrial noise exposure to the Walsh–Healey Act in May 1969. The permissible noise exposure of the regulation is given in Table 1.1.

In the United Kingdom, the Health and Safety at Work Act (1974) gives the worker the right to promote and develop measures to ensure his health and safety at work. The steady noise level should not exceed 90 dBA for an 8 h period. The Control of Pollution Act (1974) gives the local authority a wide range of powers to limit noise nuisance in its area. Many other countries have

TABLE 1.1. *Permissible noise exposure*

Maximum daily exposure (h)	Sound level (dBA)
8.0	90
6.0	92
4.0	95
3.0	97
2.0	100
1.5	102
1.0	105
0.5	110
0.25 or less	115 max

similar laws to limit noise nuisance. Consequently, there has been an increasing demand for low-noise machines, including low-noise electrical motors.

1.2. The need for low-noise electrical motors

Engineers are at present in need of more information about, and more understanding of, electrical-motor noise problems. First, more and more electrical motors are used in offices and in homes, where a high degree of quietness is demanded. Secondly, modern design resulting from, *inter alia,* competition, has tended to lead to the use of machines of a smaller weight per unit power output and hence increased electric and magnetic loadings. This leads to a relatively thin frame, higher flux densities and therefore magnetic saturation and the need for increased cooling, all leading to greater problems of noise and vibration. Sutton (1968) showed that there is a steady tendency towards a higher noise of medium-sized electric motors. The maximum octave-band sound pressure level centred at 500 Hz at a fixed point produced by three 30 kW totally-enclosed fan-cooled motors supplied by the same manufacturer for the same type of service increased from 71 dB in 1957 to 87 dB in 1967. This 'acoustic price' of progress in design could have been reduced if more understanding of noise problems had been available at the design stage.

To cope with the increasing demand for quietness of operation of electric motors, many countries have made national standards dealing with the noise measurement and/or noise limit of electric machines, i.e. motors and generators. Table 1.2 gives a list of National and International Standards relevant to electric motor noise.

1.3. Aim and composition of the book

The aim of the book is to present the basic mechanisms of noise production in electrical motors and to provide theoretical as well as experimental information about methods needed to reduce the noise emission from an electrical motor.

The fundamental acoustic terms used in motor noise measurement and the basic noise measuring methods are presented briefly in Chapter 2.

The motor noise having electromagnetic origins is mainly due to the radial forces produced by the magnetic flux density waves in the air gap. These forces will cause the motor to vibrate and emit noise to the surroundings. In order to understand the mechanism of magnetic noise generation, it is necessary to study (a) the characteristics of the radial forces, (b) the mechanical behaviour of the motor structure, and (c) the noise radiation characteristics. These are discussed in Chapters 3, 4, and 5, respectively.

To reduce the noise of magnetic origins, one can take measures to reduce the exciting magnetic forces, to reduce the vibration level of the motor and to alter the radiation characteristics. Various methods are given in Chapter 6.

TABLE 1.2. *National and International Standards on noise of electrical machines*

Nation	Identification of Standard	Name of Standard
Australia	AS 1081−1975	Measurement of airborne noise emitted by rotating electrical machinery
Bulgaria	BDS 6011−66	Measurement of noise emitted by electrical rotating machines
Czechoslavakia	CSN 35 0000	Measurement of noise emitted by electrical machines
	CSN 35 0019	Special testing methods for electrical machines, III, Noise Measurement
	CSN 36 1005	Noise measurement of domestic electrical motor-operated appliances
France	NFS 31−006 1966	Code d'essai pour la mesure de bruit émis par les machines electriques tournantes
Germany (DDR)	TGL 50−29034	Geräuschmessungen an rotierenden elektrischen Maschinen, Richtlinien
Germany (FRG)	DIN 45632	Vornorm Geräuschmessung an Maschinen, elektrischen Richtlinien
Hungary	LGSZ 40.0650−69	Rotating electrical machines Determination of the sound pressure level
India	IS: 6098−1971	Methods of measurement of the airborne noise emitted by rotating electrical machinery
Japan	JEM 1020−1965	Induction motor tests, Part 4.2 − Noise measurement
Poland	PN−72 E−04257	Electrical rotating machinery Determination of acoustic parameters of noise
Romania	STAS 7301−65	Measurement of noise emitted by electrical rotating machines
United Kingdom	BS 4999: Part 51: 1973	General requirements for rotating electrical machinery, Part 51 − Noise levels
USA	IEEE Std 85-1973	Test procedure for airborne sound measurements on rotating electric machinery
USSR	Gost 11929−66	Measurement of noise emitted by electrical rotating machines and transformers
IEC*	IEC 34−9 (1972)	Rotating electrical machines, Part 9 − Noise limits
ISO†	R1680−1970	Test code for the measurement of the airborne noise emitted by rotating electrical machinery

*International Electrotechnical Commission.
† International Organization for Standardization.

The characteristics of motor noise due to mechanical origins, e.g. bearings, brush commutators and rotor unbalance, are discussed together with the noise reduction measures in Chapter 7.

With the ever increasing cooling requirement of electrical motors, motor noise components of aerodynamic origins are sometimes the predominent noise

components, especially for large motors. Various practical methods to suppress
motor noise of aerodynamic origins are presented in Chapter 8.

References

British Standards Institution (1955). *Glossary of acoustic terms.* BS 661.
Control of Pollution Act (1974). HMSO, London.
Health and Safety at Work Act (1974). HMSO, London.
SUTTON, P. (1968). Design of a noise specification for process plant. *J. Sound
    Vib.*, 8, 33–43.

2. Electrical motor noise measurement

In this chapter we shall introduce the fundamental acoustic terms which are used in specifying the noise emission of an electrical motor and the basic methods for electrical motor noise measurement.

2.1. Sound pressure level

In order to describe the intensity of a noise, it is a well established practice to use an acoustic term called sound pressure level. The sound pressure level in decibels (dB) is defined as

$$L_p = 10 \log_{10} \frac{p^2}{p_{ref}^2} \tag{2.1}$$

where p is the r.m.s. sound pressure (N/m²) at a given point in the noise field, and p_{ref} is the reference sound pressure, which is equal to 2×10^{-5} N/m². The reference sound pressure p_{ref} of 2×10^{-5} N/m² approximates the lowest r.m.s. sound pressure audible to an average person at 1000 Hz.

2.2. Mean sound pressure level and motor noise measurement

The sound pressure levels around an electrical motor vary not only with the distance from the motor but also with the location of the measuring point (Ellison, Moore and Yang 1969) (see Fig. 2.1). Therefore, a sound pressure level value measured at any single location around a motor does not give a meaningful description of the noise emission of a motor. It is necessary to measure the sound pressure level values at a number of points on an imaginary surface enclosing the motor and to calculate the mean sound pressure level. We can then describe the noise emission of a given motor by quoting the mean sound pressure level on the measuring surface enclosing it. The mean sound pressure level in decibels is defined as

$$\bar{L}_p = 10 \log_{10} \frac{p_{av}^2}{p_{ref}^2} \tag{2.2}$$

where p_{av} is the average sound pressure on the measuring surface and p_{ref} is as previously defined.

Based on eqns. (2.1) and (2.2) the mean sound pressure level in decibels can

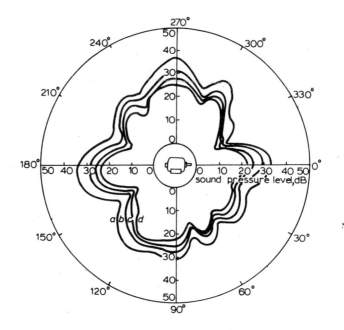

Fig. 2.1. Variations of sound pressure level along four concentric circulator paths for a pure-tone component emitted from an electrical motor (see Ellison *et al.* 1969)

Distance from motor centre   (a) 0.3 m   (b) 0.48 m   (c) 0.61 m   (d) 0.76 m

be expressed as

$$\bar{L}_{\mathrm{p}} = 10 \log_{10} \left\{ \frac{1}{n} \left(\sum_{i=1}^{n} \text{antilog}_{10} \frac{L_{\mathrm{p},\,i}}{10} \right) \right\} \tag{2.3}$$

where $L_{\mathrm{p},\,i}$ is the sound pressure at the ith measurement point and n is the total number of measurement points.

The mean sound pressure level obtained from a given motor depends on the shape and location of the measuring surface. For small electrical motors the convenient measuring surface can be a hemispherical surface with a radius of 1 m or 0.5 m and all the measurement points should be spread evenly over the surface (see Fig. 2.2). For medium-sized and large motors, it can be a surface which is at certain key points 1 m away from the motor surface. An example showing the measuring points for a large motor is given in Fig. 2.3.

In free acoustic field, e.g. in an anechoic chamber, where sound reflections are negligible, the mean sound pressure level obtained from a 0.5 m radius hemispherical surface enclosing a small motor is 6 dB greater than the mean sound level obtained from a 1 m radius hemispherical surface enclosing the same motor. Therefore, it is essential to quote the mean sound pressure level value

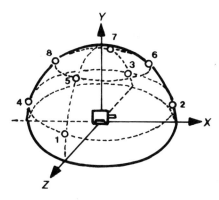

Fig. 2.2. Example of the distribution of 8 measuring points over an imaginary hemispherical surface enclosing a small motor. r = radius of hemisphere = 1 m

Location of point	X (m)	Y (m)	Z (m)
1	0	0.25	0.97
2	0.97	0.25	0
3	0	0.25	−0.97
4	−0.97	0.25	0
5	0	0.78	0.63
6	0.63	0.78	0
7	0	0.78	−0.63
8	−0.63	0.78	0

together with the shape and location of the measuring surface. When we want to compare the noise emission of two motors, we should compare the mean sound pressure level values referred to a common measuring surface. In order to avoid the need to quote both the mean sound pressure level and the shape and location of the measuring surface, we can use another acoustic term called sound power level.

2.3. Sound power level

The sound power level in decibels is defined as

$$L_W = 10 \log_{10} \frac{P}{P_{ref}} \tag{2.4}$$

where P is the sound power in watts emitted by a source and P_{ref} is the reference sound power in watts which is equal to 10^{-12} W.

The relationship between the sound power level L_W and the mean sound

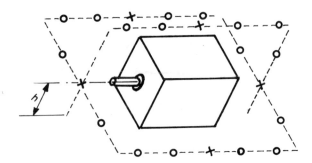

Fig. 2.3. Example of the distribution of noise measuring points for a large motor (see BS 4999 1973)

h Shaft height
× Key measuring points (1 m away from motor surface)
○ Other measuring points

pressure level $\bar{L}_p$ on a given measuring surface S is given by (Ellison *et al.* 1969)

$$L_W = \bar{L}_p + 10 \log_{10} S \tag{2.5}$$

where S is the total area of the measuring surface (m^2) and $\bar{L}_p$ is the mean sound pressure level determined by eqn. (2.3).

It should be emphasized that, in free acoustic field, the sound power level is a unique value for a given motor operating under a given condition, regardless of the location of the measuring surface. As mentioned above, the mean sound pressure level value obtained from a 0.5 m radius hemispherical surface is 6 dB greater than that from a 1 m radius hemispherical surface. However, the value of $10 \log_{10} S$ for the 0.5 m surface is 6 dB less than that for the 1 m surface. Thus, based on eqn. (2.5), the sound power levels obtained by the two different measuring surfaces are the same. We can therefore compare the sound power levels of two motors directly without mentioning the shape and location of the measuring surfaces.

2.4. Sound level and sound power level in A weighting

The human ear can sense sound waves in the frequency range from 20 Hz to 20 kHz and its sensitivity varies with frequency and sound pressure level. Fig. 2.4 shows the test results on human ear sensitivity based on the 'normal' person in the age group from 18 to 25 years. The curves in Fig. 2.4 are called 'equal

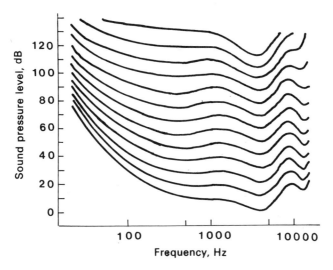

Fig. 2.4. Equal loudness contours for pure tones (the listeners are normal persons in the age group from 18 to 25 years)

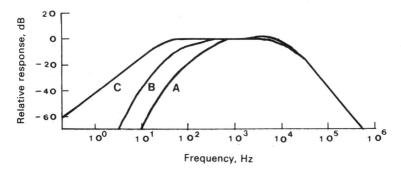

Fig. 2.5. The frequency response of A, B, and C weightings

A = A weighting
B = B weighting
C = C weighting

loudness contours' since the 'normal' person regards the pure-tone sounds having the sound pressure level values on an equal loudness contour as equally loud. For example, a 1000 Hz pure-tone sound with a sound pressure level of 20 dB is considered by the 'normal' person as equally loud as a 100 Hz pure-tone sound having a sound pressure level of 36 dB on the same equal loudness contour. In other words, the human ear attenuates the low frequency sounds and gives different weightings to sounds at different frequencies. In order to simulate the human ear frequency response, a number of frequency weightings have been

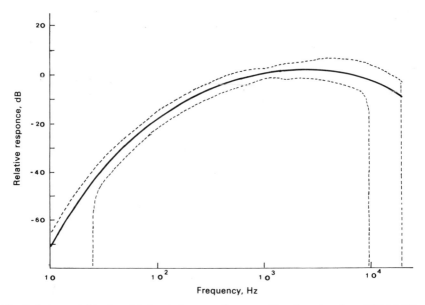

Fig. 2.6. Acceptable A weighting tolerances for sound level meters (see IEC 1961)

standardized internationally. The most common and well known weightings are A, B and C weightings and their frequency responses are shown in Fig. 2.5. All commercial noise measuring meters have A weighting, the most widely used weighting. When we use a noise meter with A weighting to measure the motor noise, which usually consists of predominant noise components at various frequencies, the sound pressure levels at different frequencies are first weighted by an A-weighting network, the frequency response of which is within the acceptable tolerance limits as shown in Fig. 2.6 (IEC 1961), and then are combined to yield a reading for the A-weighted total sound pressure level. This total sound pressure level is defined as the sound level in A weighting. It is also called A-weighted sound level. Its unit is written as dBA or dB(A).

The combination of a number of noise components at different frequencies is given by

$$p_{\text{tot}} = \left(\sum_{k=1}^{m} p_k^2 \right)^{1/2} \tag{2.6}$$

where p_k is the r.m.s. sound pressure of the kth noise component and m is the total number of the predominant noise components.

The sound level in A weighting can be expressed as

$$L_A = 10 \log_{10} \frac{p_{\text{tot, A}}^2}{p_{\text{ref}}^2}$$

$$= 10 \log_{10} \sum_{k=1}^{m} 10^{(L_{\text{p}, k, A}/10)} \tag{2.7}$$

where $p_{tot, A}$ is the A-weighted total sound pressure and $L_{p, k, A}$ is the A-weighted sound pressure level of the kth noise component.

The sound level in A weighting has been accepted as the most convenient noise scale and is used in many National and International Standards in specifying electrical motor noise emission. BS 4999 (1973) specifies the upper noise limits of rotating electrical machines in terms of the sound power level in A weighting.

The sound power level in A weighting is given by

$$L_{W, A} = \bar{L}_A + 10 \log_{10} S \qquad (2.8)$$

where S is the total area of the noise measuring surface (m²), and $\bar{L}_A$ is the mean sound level in A weighting, which can be determined by the following expression:

$$\bar{L}_A = 10 \log \left(\frac{1}{n} \sum_{i=1}^{n} antilog_{10} \frac{L_{A, i}}{10} \right) \qquad (2.9)$$

where $L_{A, i}$ is the sound level in A weighting obtained at the ith measuring point and n is the total number of measuring points.

Although the sound level and sound power level in A weighting are convenient quantities in specifying a noise, they do not provide the details of the noise characteristics. In addition to the sound level in A weighting, many noise measuring meters commercially available give the sound pressure levels in discrete standardized frequency bands or narrow-band sound pressure levels. The latter are the sound pressure levels for virtually a single frequency and are very useful in noise source identification. The most common discrete frequency bands are octave-bands and Table 1.2 gives their centre frequencies and bandwidths. The reading from an octave-band noise measuring device is called the octave-band sound pressure level. Sometimes the octave-band mean sound pressure levels or octave-band sound power levels, having centre frequencies at

TABLE 2.1. *Octave-band centre frequencies and bandwidths*

Octave-band centre frequency (Hz)	Bandwidth	
	Lower cut-off frequency (Hz)	Upper cut-off frequency (Hz)
31.5	22	44
63	44	88
125	88	177
250	177	355
500	355	710
1000	710	1420
2000	1420	2840
4000	2840	5680
8000	5680	11360

31.5, 63, 125, 250, 500, 1000, 2000, 4000, and 8000 Hz, are used to specify the
noise emission of a motor.

2.5. Accuracy in motor noise results

It should be emphasized that the mean sound pressure level and the mean sound
level in A weighting, as determined by eqns. (2.3) and (2.9), respectively, are
accurate noise results only when the following conditions are satisfied:

  (a) the noise measurements are made in a free field, e.g. in an anechoic chamber;
  (b) the noise measuring equipment has been properly calibrated; and
  (c) the number of measuring points is very large.

Many motor manufacturers can provide suitable facilities to meet the above conditions (a) and (b). However, the condition (c) can hardly be satisfied. For
economical and practical reasons, the total number of measuring points on a
measuring surface is often less than 20. The error introduced by an insufficient
number of measuring points has been studied by Ellison *et al.* (1969) and Fig.
2.7 gives the necessary correction.

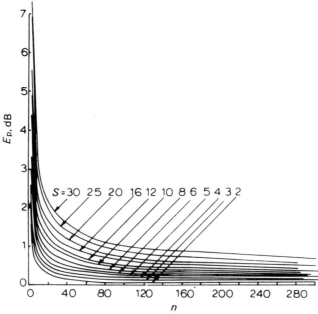

Fig. 2.7. Variation of error in mean sound pressure level with number of
measuring points and spread of sound pressure levels (see Ellison *et al.* 1969)

n Number of measuring points.
S Spread of sound pressure levels, i.e. the difference between the highest and lowest sound
   pressure levels for the n measurements.
E_p True mean sound pressure level − the measured mean sound pressure level based on n
   measurements.

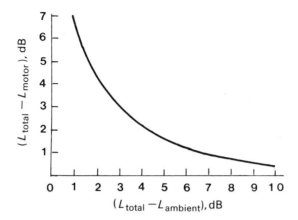

Fig. 2.8. Correction for ambient (background) noise

L_{total} Total noise level, i.e. the combination of motor noise and ambient noise levels.
$L_{ambient}$ Ambient noise level.
L_{motor} Motor noise level, i.e. the noise level without ambient noise.

If an anechoic chamber is not available, the noise measurements can be made in an ordinary large room. The noise reading taken in a large room is the reading for the combination of the direct motor noise, the ambient noise and the reflected noise due to room reflection. According to BS 4999 (1973), the room suitability for noise measurements can be checked by placing a small broad-band noise source (preferably non-aerodynamic) at the position to be occupied by the geometrical centre of the motor to be tested, and determining the mean sound level in A weighting (or the mean sound pressure levels for each frequency band concerned) at the noise measurement positions and at corresponding positions at half their distance from the source. The difference between these mean sound levels (or these mean sound pressure levels) at full and half distances should be at least 5 dB. This ensures that the contribution due to room reflection at the measurement positions is on average less than 1 dB. The correction for ambient noise is given in Fig. 2.8.

It should be pointed out that the accuracy of eqn. (2.5) for the sound power level is established on the following assumptions: (a) the sound pressure and particle velocity of the noise field are in phase with each other at every point of measurement, and (b) the particle velocity is equal to $p/\rho c$, where p is the sound pressure, ρ is the air density and c is the speed of sound in air. However, it has been shown (Yang 1975; Ellison and Yang 1971) that there is a considerable phase angle between the sound pressure and particle velocity for the magnetic noise field around a motor. Furthermore, the particle velocity is not equal to $p/\rho c$. Thus the sound power level determined by eqn. (2.5) may be erroneous. Based on Yang's analytical results (1975), the following simple guide can be used to avoid a significant error in the sound power level result. One should check the value of $(\omega/c)r$, where ω is the angular frequency concerned (note $\omega = 2\pi f$) in rad/s, c is the speed of sound in air (m/s), and r is the radius of noise measurement (m). If the $(\omega/c)r$ value is greater than 5, the error in the sound power level result is usually small. If the value of $(\omega/c)r$ is less than 3, the error in the sound power level can be significant. One should then use a larger radius of noise measurement so that the $(\omega/c)r$ value becomes greater than 5.

The noise emission from a motor, in general, varies with the load, the supply voltage and frequency, and the mounting and coupling conditions. For the purposes of noise tests, BS 4999 (1973) recommends that the following conditions should be observed:

(a) The motor shall be run on no load. Synchronous motors shall be run at unity power factor.

(b) The machine shall be in its fully assembled condition, and uncoupled.

(c) A.C. machines shall be supplied at rated voltage and frequency.

(d) Motors shall be run as near as possible to rated speed, or at the highest speed in the speed range.

(e) Motors designed to operate at two or more discrete speeds shall be tested at each speed.

References

British Standards Institution (1973). Noise levels (Part of BS 4999, General requirements for rotating electrical machinery). BS 4999: Part 51.

ELLISON, A.J., MOORE, C.J. and YANG, S.J. (1969). Methods of measurement of acoustic noise radiated by an electric machine. *Proc. Instn. Elect. Engrs.* **116**, 1419–31.

ELLISON, A.J. and YANG, S.J. (1971). Calculation of acoustic power radiated by an electrical machine. *Acustica* **25**, 28–34.

IEC (1961). *Recommendations for sound level meters.* IEC Publication 123.

YANG, S.J. (1975). Effect of length-diameter ratio on noise radiation from an electrical machine. *Acustica* **32**, 255–61.

3. Magnetic exciting forces

3.1. Introduction

The main magnetic flux in an electrical machine passes across the air gap in an approximately radial direction and produces radial forces on stator and rotor, hence magnetic noise and vibrations and the tangential forces which give rise to the working electromagnetic torque and tangential vibrations. Great efforts have been made to calculate accurately the magnetic flux distribution in the air gap. There are two different approaches to the problem: (i) the flux distribution is calculated as the result of multiplying the expression for the m.m.f. distribution of the winding by that for the permeance of the air gap, or (ii) the flux distribution is calculated by conformal transformation, a finite difference method or a finite element method, considering the slotted nature of the boundaries of the stator and rotor slots. The finite element method and finite difference method are both well adapted to finding the flux distribution in a machine allowing for iron saturation. Binns (1968) points out that the first approach gives only an approximation to the true flux distribution, and, where permeance and m.m.f. harmonics of similar order are involved, the accuracy to be expected is not high. However, so far as the predominant magnetic noise components are concerned, the most important harmonic components of the m.m.f. waves are usually large compared with a slot pitch. Furthermore, in the present state of the art, there are a number of areas, e.g. the damping capacity and the dynamic deflection, for which we have insufficient knowledge to make an accurate calculation. The following study, therefore, will follow the permeance approach for simplicity and clarity.

3.2. Permeance waves and m.m.f. waves

The permeance wave of the air gap results, generally, from the presence of the following: (a) the rotor slots, (b) the stator slots, (c) eccentricity of, and dissymmetries in, stator and rotor, and (d) magnetic saturation. The permeance Λ of an air gap bounded by a slotted stator and a smooth rotor is given by

$$\Lambda_{st}(\phi) = \sum_{i_{st}=0}^{\infty} \Lambda_{i_{st}} \cos(i_{st} Z_{st} \phi) \qquad (3.1)$$

where ϕ is the angular position, Z_{st} the stator slot number and i_{st} an integer.

The permeance of an air gap bounded by a slotted rotor and a smooth stator is given by

$$\Lambda_{rt}(\phi, t) = \sum_{i_{rt}=0}^{\infty} \Lambda_{i_{rt}} \cos\{i_{rt}Z_{rt}(\phi - \omega_{rt}t)\} \tag{3.2}$$

where Z_{rt} is the rotor slot number, i_{rt} an integer and ω_{rt} the rotor angular speed (rad/s). The total reluctance R of the air gap when both stator and rotor are slotted is expressed as

$$R_{st, rt} = \frac{1}{\Lambda_{st}} + \frac{1}{\Lambda_{rt}} - \frac{1}{\Lambda_g} \tag{3.3}$$

where $\Lambda_g = \mu_0/g$, g is the mean air-gap length and μ_0 is the permeability of free space. The corresponding total permeance can be expressed by

$$\Lambda_{st, rt} = \frac{1}{R_{st, rt}} = \frac{\Lambda_{st}\Lambda_{rt}\Lambda_g}{\Lambda_{rt}\Lambda_g + \Lambda_{st}\Lambda_g - \Lambda_{rt}\Lambda_{st}}. \tag{3.4}$$

The denominator in the above equation contains a constant component and a series of variable components. The variable components are small in comparison with the constant component and may be neglected. Eqn (3.4) thus reduces to

$$\Lambda_{st, rt} \simeq k\Lambda_{st}\Lambda_{rt} \tag{3.5}$$

where k is a coefficient having dimensions of (units of permeance)$^{-1}$.

Therefore, the resultant permeance of these two permeances in parallel can be expressed approximately as the product of a coefficient and the values of the two permeances. The air-gap permeance when both stator and rotor are slotted is approximately given by

$$\Lambda_{st, rt}(\phi, t) = \sum_{i_{st}=0}^{\infty} \sum_{i_{rt}=0}^{\infty} k'_{i_{st}, i_{rt}} \overbrace{\cos(i_{st}Z_{st}\phi)}^{A} \overbrace{\cos\{i_{rt}Z_{rt}(\phi - \omega_{rt}t)\}}^{B}$$

$$= \sum_{i_{st}=0}^{\infty} \sum_{i_{rt}=0}^{\infty} \Lambda_{i_{st}, i_{rt}} \cos\{(i_{rt}Z_{rt} \pm i_{st}Z_{st})\phi - i_{rt}Z_{rt}\omega_{rt}t\}. \tag{3.6}$$

The air-gap permeance due to dynamic rotor eccentricity and dissymmetries of the rotor shape is

$$\Lambda_{ec, rtd}(\phi, t) = \sum_{i_{ec, rtd}=0}^{\infty} \Lambda_{i_{ec, rtd}} \cos i_{ec, rtd}(\phi - \omega_{ec}t) \tag{3.7}$$

where $i_{ec, rtd}$ is an integer and ω_{ec} the dynamic rotor angular speed (rad/s).

If the rotor is closely cylindrical and sufficiently rigid so that the variations in the air-gap length under running condition are negligible, the air-gap permeance due to the static rotor eccentricity is

$$\Lambda_{ec, rts}(\phi) = \sum_{i_{ec, rts}=0}^{\infty} \Lambda_{i_{ec, rts}} \cos(i_{ec, rts}\phi) \tag{3.8}$$

where $i_{ec, rts}$ is an integer.

Combining eqns (3.8) and (3.7) by the same method used for obtaining eqn (3.6)

$$\Lambda_{ec, rtd, ec, rts}(\phi, t) = \sum_{i_{ec, rtd}=0}^{\infty} \sum_{i_{ec, rts}=0}^{\infty} \Lambda_{i_{ec, rtd}, i_{ec, rts}}$$

$$\cos\{(i_{ec, rtd} \pm i_{ec, rts}) \phi - i_{ec, rtd}\omega_{ec} t\}. \quad (3.9)$$

Dissymmetries in the stator shape give rise to the following permeance:

$$\Lambda_{ec, st}(\phi) = \sum_{i_{ec, st}=0}^{\infty} \Lambda_{i_{ec, st}} \cos(i_{ec, st}\phi) \quad (3.10)$$

where $i_{ec, st}$ is an integer.

Combining the permeance due to stator dissymmetries and the permeance due to dynamic and stator rotor eccentricity and rotor dissymmetries in the way in which the stator slots permeance and rotor slots permeance waves were combined, the following expression results:

$$\Lambda_{ec}(\phi, t) = \sum_{i_{ec, rts}=0}^{\infty} \sum_{i_{ec, rtd}=0}^{\infty} \sum_{i_{ec, st}=0}^{\infty} \Lambda_{i_{ec, rtd}, i_{ec, st}, i_{ec, rts}}$$

$$\cos\{(i_{ec, rtd} \pm i_{ec, st} \pm i_{ec, rts})\phi - i_{ec, rtd}\omega_{ec} t\}. \quad (3.11)$$

The effect of saturation can be represented by a fluctuation in the permeance of the air gap (Harlin 1965; Randell 1965). Tooth saturation is represented by an air gap which varies in both space and time. This air gap becomes larger in the regions of maximum flux density and has twice the number of pole pairs and twice the frequency of the fundamental wave. The permeance of a smooth and concentric air gap combined with the effect of saturation is thus expressed as (Harlin 1965)

$$\Lambda_{sa}(\phi, t) = \sum_{i_{sa}=0}^{\infty} \Lambda_{i_{sa}} \cos\{i_{sa}(2p\phi - 2\omega_1 t)\} \quad (3.12)$$

where i_{sa} is an integer, p the pole pair number and ω_1 the fundamental angular frequency (rad/s).

Combining eqns (3.11) and (3.12) by the same method used for obtaining eqn (3.6), the permeance waves due to dissymmetries, eccentricity and saturation are given by

$$\Lambda_{ec, sa}(\phi, t) = \sum_{i_{ec, rts}=0}^{\infty} \sum_{i_{ec, rtd}=0}^{\infty} \sum_{i_{ec, st}=0}^{\infty} \sum_{i_{sa}=0}^{\infty} \Lambda_{i_{ec, rts}, i_{ec, rtd}, i_{ec, st}, i_{sa}}$$

$$\cos\{(i_{ec, rtd} \pm i_{ec, st} \pm i_{ec, rts} \pm 2i_{sa}p)\phi - (i_{ec, rtd}\omega_{ec} \pm 2i_{sa}\omega_1)t\} \quad (3.13)$$

Similarly, by combining eqns (3.6) and (3.13), the total permeance waves in the air gap, taking stator and rotor slotting, eccentricity, dissymmetries, and iron saturation into account, are expressed as follows:

$$\Lambda_{tot}(\phi, t) =$$

$$\sum_{i_{st}=0}^{\infty} \sum_{i_{rt}=0}^{\infty} \sum_{i_{ec, st}=0}^{\infty} \sum_{i_{ec, rtd}=0}^{\infty} \sum_{i_{ec, rts}=0}^{\infty} \sum_{i_{sa}=0}^{\infty} \Lambda_{i_{st}, i_{rt}, i_{ec, st}, i_{ec, rtd}, i_{ec, rts}, i_{sa}}$$

$$\cos\{(i_{rt}Z_{rt} \pm i_{st}Z_{st} \pm i_{ec, rtd} \pm i_{ec, rts} \pm 2i_{sa}p \pm i_{ec, st})\phi$$

$$- (i_{rt}Z_{rt}\omega_{rt} \pm i_{ec, rtd}\omega_{ec} \pm 2i_{sa}\omega_1)t\}. \tag{3.14}$$

It is well known that the flow of current in an ordinary winding of an electric machine produces a series of space harmonic m.m.f. waves in addition to the fundamental. The analysis of the resultant wave form is to be found in many electric machinery textbooks.

The stator m.m.f. is given by

$$F_{st} = \sum_{k_{st}=1}^{\infty} \sum_{q_{st}=-\infty}^{\infty} F_{k_{st}q_{st}} \cos\left\{k_{st}p\left(\phi - \frac{\alpha_{st}z}{l_c}\right) - q_{st}\omega_1 t - \psi_{k_{st}, q_{st}}\right\} \tag{3.15}$$

where α_{st} is the angle of skew of the stator slots, k is the order of a space harmonic and may take the positive integral value, and q is the order of the current time harmonics and may take any positive or negative integral values corresponding to the direction of rotation of the wave ($q = 0$ corresponding to a d.c. condition), l_c is the core length, z is the axial distance from the centre of the machine and ψ is the phase angle.

The rotor m.m.f. referred to the stator side for a.c. machines can be expressed as

$$F_{rt} = \sum_{k_{rt}=1}^{\infty} \sum_{q_{rt}=-\infty}^{\infty} F_{k_{rt}, q_{rt}}$$

$$\cos\left\{k_{rt}p\left(\phi - \omega_{rt}t - \frac{\alpha_{rt}z}{l_c}\right) - q_{rt}s\omega_1 t - \psi_{k_{rt}, q_{rt}}\right\} \tag{3.16}$$

where α_{rt} is the angle of skew of the rotor slots and s is the slip.

The magnitude, F, and the order of the harmonics, k and q, depend on the number of phases, the number and shape of the slots, the arrangement of the conductors in the winding, the iron properties and the applied waveform and are dealt with elsewhere (Liwschitz-Garik and Whipple 1946; Chalmers 1965).

The resultant m.m.f. pattern is obtained by summing eqns (3.15) and (3.16) as follows:

$$F_{\text{tot}} = \sum_{k_{st}=1}^{\infty} \sum_{q_{st}=-\infty}^{\infty} F_{k_{st}, q_{st}}$$

$$\cos \{k_{st}p\phi - q_{st}\omega_1 t - k_{st}\alpha_{st}zp/l_c - \psi_{k_{st}, q_{st}}\}$$

$$+ \sum_{k_{rt}=1}^{\infty} \sum_{q_{rt}=-\infty}^{\infty} F_{k_{st}, q_{rt}}$$

$$\cos \{k_{rt}p\phi - (q_{rt}s\omega_1 + k_{rt}p\omega_{rt})t - k_{rt}p\alpha_{rt}z/l_c - \psi_{k_{rt}, q_{rt}}\}. \tag{3.17}$$

3.3. Electromagnetic force waves

The magnetic flux density waves in the air gap are taken as the product of the permeance waves and m.m.f. waves set out earlier. Multiplying eqns (3.17) and (3.14) we obtain the following expression for the flux density in the air gap:

$$B(\phi, t, z) = \sum_{m_{ist}, \, \omega_{ist}} B_{m_{ist}, \, \omega_{ist}} \cos \{m_{ist}\phi - \omega_{ist}t \pm (k_{st}\alpha_{st}zp/l_c + \psi_{k_{st}, q_{rt}})\}$$

$$+ \sum_{m_{irt}, \, \omega_{irt}} B_{m_{irt}, \, \omega_{irt}} \cos \{m_{irt}\phi - \omega_{irt}t \pm (k_{rt}\alpha_{rt}zp/l_c + \psi_{k_{rt}, q_{rt}})\} \tag{3.18}$$

where

$$m_{ist} = i_{rt}Z_{rt} \pm i_{st}Z_{st} \pm i_{ec, \, rts} \pm i_{ec, \, rtd} \pm 2i_{sa}p \pm i_{ec, \, st} \pm k_{st}p$$

$$\omega_{ist} = i_{rt}Z_{rt}\omega_{rt} \pm i_{ec, \, rtd}\omega_{ec} \pm 2i_{sa}\omega_1 \pm q_{st}\omega_1$$

$$m_{irt} = i_{rt}Z_{rt} \pm i_{st}Z_{st} \pm i_{ec, \, rts} \pm i_{ec, \, rtd} \pm 2i_{sa}p \pm i_{ec, \, st} \pm k_{rt}p$$

$$\omega_{irt} = i_{rt}Z_{rt}\omega_{rt} \pm i_{ec, \, rtd}\omega_{ec} \pm 2i_{sa}\omega_1 \pm q_{rt}\omega_1 \pm k_{rt}p\omega_{rt}$$

The radial force wave σ_{ra} value is proportional at every point to the square of the flux density wave (Seely 1962)

$$\sigma_{ra}(\phi, t, z) = \frac{B^2(\phi, t, z)}{2\mu_0} \tag{3.19}$$

where σ_{ra} is the force per unit area (N/m^2).

Substituting eqn (3.18) into eqn (3.19) and neglecting the effects of skew and the phase angles ψ in eqn (3.18), we have

$$\sigma_{ra}(\phi, t) = \sum_{m_i, \, \omega_i} \sigma_{m_i, \, \omega_i} \cos (m_i\phi - \omega_i t) \tag{3.20}$$

where

$$m_i = i'_{rt}Z_{rt} \pm i'_{st}Z_{st} \pm k'p \pm 2i'_{sa}p \pm i'_{ec, \, rtd} \pm i'_{ec, \, st} \pm i'_{ec, \, rts}$$

$$\omega_i = i'_{rt}Z_{rt}\omega_{rt} \pm (q' + 2i'_{sa})\omega_1 \pm i'_{ec, \, rtd}\omega_{ec}$$

where the primed symbols denote the sum or difference of any two similar quantities, i.e.

$$i'_{rt} = i_{rt, \, 1} \pm i_{rt, \, 2}$$

$$i'_{st} = i_{st, \, 1} \pm i_{st, \, 2}$$

$$i'_{sa} = i_{sa, \, 1} \pm i_{sa, \, 2}$$

$$i'_{ec, \, rtd} = i_{ec, \, rtd, \, 1} \pm i_{ec, \, rtd, \, 2}$$

$$i'_{ec, \, rts} = i_{ec, \, rts, \, 1} \pm i_{ec, \, rts, \, 2}$$

$$i'_{ec, \, st} = i_{ec, \, st, \, 1} \pm i_{ec, \, st, \, 2}$$

$$k' = (k_{st, \, 1} \pm k_{st, \, 2})$$

or

$$(k_{st, \, 1} \pm k_{rt, \, 2})$$

or

$$(k_{rt, \, 1} \pm k_{rt, \, 2})$$

and

$$q' = (q_{st, \, 1} \pm q_{st, \, 2})$$

or

$$\left\{q_{st, \, 1} \pm \left(q_{rt, \, 2}s + k_{rt, \, 2}p\frac{\omega_{rt}}{\omega_1}\right)\right\}$$

or

$$\left\{(q_{rt, \, 1} \pm q_{rt, \, 2})s + (k_{rt, \, 1} \pm k_{rt, \, 2})p\frac{\omega_{rt}}{\omega_1}\right\}.$$

Eqn (3.20) represents a series of rotating radial force waves having various mode number m values at different frequencies. From the point of view of noise emission, the most important force waves are those which satisfy the following conditions:

(a) the amplitude of the force waves are large, compared with other force waves;

(b) the mode number m values are low, e.g. less than 10 in most cases.

Other things being equal, a higher force amplitude would cause a larger vibration amplitude to emit more noise. The second condition is based on the noise radiation characteristics discussed in Chapter 5. The main feature is that the noise radiation efficiency becomes very poor for surface vibrations with high mode number values.

If we neglect the effects of slotting, eccentricity, saturation, and stator/rotor dissymmetry, and consider only the fundamental flux, then all i' values in eqn (3.20) are equal to zero and $k' = 2$ and $q' = 2$. Thus eqn (3.20) becomes

$$\sigma_{ra}(\phi, t) = \sigma_{m_i=2p, \, \omega_i=2\omega_1} \cos(2p\phi - 2\omega_1 t) \qquad (3.21)$$

This force wave is produced by the fundamental flux and cannot be eliminated by making the machine free from any imperfections, e.g. eccentricity, stator/rotor dissymmetry and saturation. The force mode number m is twice the pole pair number p and the force frequency is twice the supply frequency. This force usually does not cause a predominant airborne noise component for a small electrical machine as its noise radiation efficiency at this frequency is relatively poor. However, for large turbogenerators this force often gives rise to an important noise and vibration component.

If we consider only the interaction of the fundamental stator/rotor slot permeance waves with the fundamental m.m.f. wave, we put $i'_{rt} = 1$, $i'_{st} = 1$, $k' = 2$, $q' = 2$ and the rest of i' values in eqn (3.20) equal to zero. Thus eqn (3.20) becomes

$$\sigma(\phi, t) = \sigma_{i'_{rt}=1, \, i'_{st}=1} \cos\{(Z_{rt} \pm Z_{st} \pm 2p)\phi - (Z_{rt}\omega_{rt} \pm 2\omega_1)t\} \qquad (3.22)$$

These force waves produce the noise and vibration components with the mode number values of $(Z_{rt} \pm Z_{st} \pm 2p)$ and the frequency values of $(Z_{rt}\omega_{rt} \pm 2\omega_1)$. For an induction machine the force frequency values in hertz are

$$f = \frac{f_1 Z_{rt}(1-s)}{p} \pm 2f_1 \qquad (3.23)$$

where s is the slip and f_1 is the fundamental supply frequency (Hz). Usually, the force waves with the mode number values of $(Z_{rt} + Z_{st} \pm 2p)$ are very much less important than those with the mode number values of $(Z_{rt} - Z_{st} \pm 2p)$ as the radiation efficiency of the former is much poorer than that of the latter.

Example 3.1

A 3-phase 50 Hz 4-pole induction machine has 44 rotor slots and 36 stator slots. Find the mode number and frequency values of the magnetic force components caused by the interaction of the fundamental m.m.f. and the fundamental stator/rotor slot permeance on no load.

Solution

Based on eqn (3.22) the force mode number values are

$$m = (Z_{rt} - Z_{st} \pm 2p) = \{44 - 36 \pm 2(2)\} = 4 \text{ or } 12$$

and

$$m = (Z_{rt} + Z_{st} \pm 2p) = \{44 + 36 \pm 2(2)\} = 76 \text{ or } 84.$$

From eqn (3.23) the force frequency values are

$$f = \frac{f_1 Z_{rt}(1-s)}{p} \pm 2f_1 = \frac{50(44)(1-0)}{2} \pm 2(50)$$

$$= 1000 \text{ Hz or } 1200 \text{ Hz (if } s \simeq 0).$$

The effect of static rotor eccentricity on the radial force waves can be explained by the following example for a 3-phase 50 Hz 4-pole induction machine having 36 stator slots and 44 rotor slots.

The fundamental static eccentricity permeance wave is obtained by putting $i_{ec, rts} = 1$ in eqn (3.8):

$$\Lambda_{i_{ec, rts}=1}(\phi) = \Lambda_{i_{ec, rts}=1} \cos \phi \tag{3.24}$$

The fundamental stator–rotor permeance expression is obtained from eqn (3.6) by putting $i_{st} = 1$ and $i_{rt} = 1$:

$$\Lambda_{i_{st}=1, i_{rt}=1}(\phi, t) = \Lambda_{i_{st}=1, i_{rt}=1} \cos \{(44 \pm 36)\phi - 44\omega_{rt}t\}. \tag{3.25}$$

Combining these two permeances in the way in which the stator slot and rotor slot permeances were combined, we have

$$\Lambda_{i_{ec, rts}=i_{st}=i_{rt}=1}(\phi, t) = \Lambda_{i_{ec, rts}=i_{rt}=i_{st}=1} \cos \{(44 \pm 36 \pm 1)\phi - 44\omega_{rt}t\}. \tag{3.26}$$

Multiplying this expression by the fundamental m.m.f. wave expression, i.e. $F_1 = \hat{F}_1 \cos (2\phi - \omega_1 t)$, the resulting flux density waves are

$$B(\phi, t) = \frac{\hat{F}_1}{2} \Lambda_{i_{ec, rts}=i_{rt}=i_{st}=1} \cos \{(44 \pm 36 \pm 1 \pm 2)\phi - (44\omega_{rt} \pm \omega_1)t\}. \tag{3.27}$$

This expression gives a number of flux density waves, including one at 1150 Hz with 9 pole pairs, assuming the slip value s to be negligible. Note that the force mode number can also be called the force pole pair number since a force wave represented by

$$\sigma(\phi, t) = \sigma_{m_i, \omega_i} \cos (m_i\phi - \omega_i t)$$

is, at a given instant, a force pattern varying along the air gap sinusoidally with m_i pole pairs.

By multiplying the fundamental static eccentricity permeance wave expression, i.e. eqn (3.24) by the 5th space harmonic m.m.f. wave, i.e. $F_5 = \hat{F}_5 \cos (10\phi + \omega_1 t)$, we obtain the following flux density waves:

$$B(\phi, t) = \frac{\hat{F}_5}{2} \Lambda_{i_{ec, rts}=1} \cos \{(10 \pm 1)\phi + \omega_1 t\}. \tag{3.28}$$

This expression gives a flux density wave with 11 pole pairs at 50 Hz (if $f_1 = 50$ Hz) rotating in the negative direction with respect to the main flux density wave. By tradition, we define a wave of $\cos (m_i\phi - \omega_i t)$ as rotating in the positive direction and a wave of $\cos (m_i\phi + \omega_i t)$ as rotating in the negative direction.

Based on eqn (3.19), force waves are produced by the multiplication of any two flux density waves. Multiplying the 11 pole pair flux wave at 50 Hz by the 9 pole pair flux wave at 1150 Hz, a force wave with two pole pairs at 1200 Hz

TABLE 3.1. *Characteristics of important flux density waves related to eccentricity (3-phase 4-pole 50 Hz induction motor) see Ellison and Yang (1971)*

Frequency* (Hz)	Number of pole pairs m	Origins					
		$\hat{F}_1$	$\hat{F}_5$	$\Lambda(i_{st}=1, i_{rt}=1)$	$\Lambda(i_{ec,\,rt}=1)$	$\Lambda(i_{sa}=1)$	$\Lambda(i_{sa}=2)$
50	1	✓			✓		
50	3	✓			✓		
50	3	✓			✓	✓	
50	1	✓			✓	✓	
−50	9		✓		✓		
−50	11		✓		✓		
150	5	✓			✓		✓
150	5	✓			✓	✓	
150	7	✓			✓	✓	
−150	9	✓			✓		✓
−250	7	✓			✓		✓
250	11	✓			✓		✓
950	3	✓		✓	✓	✓	
1050	7	✓		✓	✓	✓	
1050	9	✓		✓	✓		
1150	5	✓		✓	✓		
1150	7	✓		✓	✓		
1150	11	✓		✓	✓	✓	
1250	15	✓		✓	✓	✓	

*Sign indicates the direction of rotation of wave.
†F_1 = fundamental m.m.f.
F_s = 5th harmonic m.m.f.
$\Lambda(i_{st}=1, i_{rt}=1)$ = fundamental stator–rotor slots permeance.
$\Lambda(i_{ec,\,rt}=1)$ = fundamental eccentricity permeance.
$\Lambda(i_{sa}=1)$ = fundamental saturation permeance.

rotating in the negative direction is obtained.

From similar analyses, other force waves related to static rotor eccentricity can be obtained (Ellison and Yang 1971). Table 3.1 gives the characteristics of the flux density waves which are related to static rotor eccentricity and Table 3.2 shows the characteristics of radial force waves varying with static rotor eccentricity and having low pole pair numbers. These analytical force components caused by static rotor eccentricity were confirmed by noise measurements (Ellison and Yang 1971) and Fig. 3.1 shows the variation of these noise components with static rotor eccentricity for the machine.

The effect of dynamic rotor eccentricity on radial force waves can be studied in a similar way as the effect of static rotor eccentricity was, described above. The difference is that instead of using eqn (3.8), eqn (3.7) should be used in the analysis.

TABLE 3.2. *Characteristics of low pole-pair radial force waves related to eccentricity (3-phase 4-pole 50 Hz induction motor) see Ellison and Yang (1971)*

Frequency* (Hz)	Number of pole pair m	Origins					
		Fundamental m.m.f. $\hat{F}_1$	5th harmonic m.m.f. $\hat{F}_5$	Fundamental stator/rotor slot permeance $\Lambda(i_{st}=1, i_{rt}=1)$	Fundamental eccentricity permeance $\Lambda(i_{ec,\,rt}=1)$	Fundamental saturation permeance $\Lambda(i_{sa}=1)$	2nd harmonic saturation permeance $\Lambda(i_{sa}=2)$
−900	2	✓					
900	2	✓		✓	✓	✓	
1000	2	✓		✓	✓	✓	
1000	4	✓		✓	✓	✓	
1100	2	✓	✓	✓	✓		
1200	2	✓	✓	✓	✓		
−1200	2	✓	✓	✓	✓		
1300	4	✓			✓	✓	
1400	4	✓					✓

*Sign indicates the direction of rotation of wave.

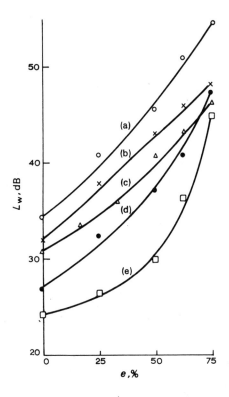

Fig. 3.1. Variation of narrow-band sound power level L_W with relative eccentricity e (Ellison and Yang 1971)

(a) 1200 Hz   (b) 1000 Hz   (c) 1300 Hz   (d) 1100 Hz   (e) 1400 Hz

3.4. Effects of homopolar flux waves in 2-pole machines

Static and dynamic eccentricity, also permeance variations in the stator and rotor cores, may introduce homopolar flux density waves in some electrical machines. These homopolar flux waves pass through the air gap and complete their paths through the stator frame, the endshields, and shaft, and back to the stator/rotor core. Part of the homopolar flux waves may return to the stator/rotor core through paths which are mainly in air. For a 2-pole single-phase induction machine the homopolar flux density waves are (Yang 1975) (see Appendix 3.1)

$$B_h(t) = \epsilon \frac{\Lambda_1'}{2} F_f \cos (s\omega_1 t) + \epsilon' \frac{\Lambda_1'}{2} F_b \cos \{(2-s)\omega_1 t\}$$

$$+ \epsilon'' \frac{\Lambda_1}{2} (F_f + F_b) \cos (\omega_1 t) \qquad (3.29)$$

where F_f and F_b are the amplitude of the forward and backward m.m.f. waves, respectively, and ϵ, ϵ' and ϵ'' are coefficients as explained in Appendix 3.1. From eqn (3.18) the general expression for the conventional non-homopolar flux density waves can be expressed as

$$B_{nh}(\phi, t) = \sum_{m_i, \, \omega_i} B_{m_i, \, \omega_i} \cos{(m_i\phi - \omega_i t + \psi_{m_i, \, \omega_i})} \qquad (3.30)$$

where

$$m_i = i_{rt}Z_{rt} \pm i_{st}Z_{st} \pm i_{ec, \, rts} \pm i_{ec, \, rtd} \pm i_{ec, \, st} \pm 2i_{sa}p \pm (k_{st} \text{ or } k_{rt})p$$

and

$$\omega_i = i_{rt}Z_{rt}\omega_{rt} \pm i_{ec, \, rtd}\omega_{ec} \pm 2i_{sa}\omega_1 \pm \left\{ q_{st} \text{ or } \left(q_{rt}s + k_{rt}p\frac{\omega_{rt}}{\omega_1} \right) \right\} \omega_1.$$

The radial force waves are equal to

$$\sigma_{ra}(\phi, t) = \frac{\{B_h(t) + B_{nh}(\phi, t)\}^2}{2\mu_0}. \qquad (3.31)$$

Combining eqns (3.30), (3.31) and (3.32), and neglecting the phase angles, the radial force waves in a 2-pole single-phase machine are as follows:

$$\sigma_{ra}(\phi, t) = \frac{1}{4\mu_0} \, [\Sigma B^2_{m_i, \, \omega_i}\{1 + \cos{(2m_i\phi - 2\omega_i t)}\}$$

$$+ 2\Sigma\Sigma B_{m_i\omega_i, \, 1}B_{m_i\omega_i, \, 2} \cos{\{(m_{i, \, 1} \pm m_{i, \, 2})\phi - (\omega_{i, \, 1} - \omega_{i, \, 2})t\} + 4\mu_0\sigma_{ra, \, h}(t)}$$

$$+ \Sigma\epsilon''\Lambda_1(F_f + F_b)B_{m_i, \, \omega_i} \cos{\{m_i\phi - (\omega_i \pm \omega_1)t\}}$$

$$- \Sigma\epsilon'\Lambda_1'F_bB_{m_i, \, \omega_i} \cos{\{m_i\phi - \omega_i t \pm (2 + s)\omega_1 t\}}$$

$$+ \Sigma\epsilon'\Lambda_1'F_bB_{m_i, \, \omega_i}\{2 + 2\cos{(2s\omega_1 t)}\}^{1/2} \cos{\{m_i\phi - \omega_1 t \pm 2\omega_1 t\}}$$

$$+ \Sigma\epsilon\Lambda_1'F_fB_{m_i, \, \omega_i}\{2 + 2\cos{(2s\omega_1 t)}\}^{1/2} \cos{(m_i\phi - \omega_i t)}] \qquad (3.32)$$

The first two terms in eqn (3.32) represent the radial force waves produced by the conventional non-homopolar flux density waves and the rest of eqn (3.32) represents the additional radial force waves introduced by the homopolar flux density waves alone, i.e. $\sigma_{ra, \, h}(t)$, and by the interaction of the homopolar and non-homopolar flux density waves. The last two terms of eqn (3.32) give a series of radial force waves having an amplitude pulsating at twice the slip frequency. These pulsating forces produce a noise which pulsates in magnitude.

With the aid of eqn (3.32) it is possible to predict the frequencies of those noise components having pulsating amplitudes from the main design data of a machine. For example, for a small 2-pole 50 Hz single-phase machine having 12 stator slots and 22 rotor slots, the frequencies and origins of the important

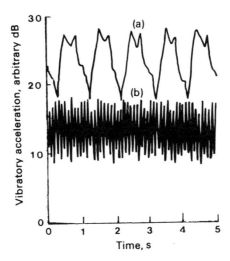

Fig. 3.2. Narrow-band vibratory acceleration on surface of a 2-pole motor (Yang 1975)

(a) 1039 Hz, speed = 2970 r/min.
(b) 1230 Hz, speed = 2700 r/min.

pulsating radial force waves when running at 2970 r/min and 2700 r/min can be found from this equation and are given in Table 3.3. All these pulsating force components were verified by noise and vibration measurements (see Figs. 3.2 and 3.3).

For a 2-pole 3-phase machine operating under balanced conditions, the homopolar flux waves are (see Appendix 3.1)

$$B_h(t) = \epsilon \frac{\Lambda_1'}{2} F_f \cos(s\omega_1 t) + \epsilon'' \frac{\Lambda_1}{2} F_f \cos(\omega_1 t) \qquad (3.33)$$

Combining eqns (3.33), (3.30), and (3.31) and neglecting the phase angles, the radial force waves in a 2-pole 3-phase machine are given by

$$\sigma_{ra}(\phi, t) = \frac{1}{4\mu_0} [\Sigma B_{m_i, \omega_i}^2 \{1 + \cos(2m_i\phi - 2\omega_i t)\}$$

$$+ 2\Sigma\Sigma B_{m_i, \omega_i, 1} B_{m_i, \omega_i, 2} \cos\{(m_{i,1} \pm m_{i,2})\phi - (\omega_{i,1} \pm \omega_{i,2})t\}$$

$$+ \tfrac{1}{4}\epsilon^2 \Lambda_1'^2 F_f^2 \{1 + \cos(2s\omega_1 t)\} + \tfrac{1}{4}\epsilon'' \Lambda_1^2 F_f^2 \{1 + \cos(2\omega_1 t)\}$$

$$+ \Sigma\epsilon'' \Lambda_1 F_f B_{m_i, \omega_i} \cos\{m_i\phi - (\omega_i \pm \omega_1)t\}$$

$$+ \tfrac{1}{2}\epsilon\epsilon'' \Lambda_1' \Lambda_1 F_f^2 \cos\{(1 \pm s)\omega_1 t\}$$

$$+ \Sigma\epsilon\Lambda_1' F_f B_{m_i, \omega_i} \{2 + 2\cos(2s\omega_1 t)\}^{1/2} \cos(m_i\phi - \omega_i t)]. \quad (3.34)$$

TABLE 3.3. *Characteristics of important pulsating radial force waves for a 2-pole single-phase machine* (Yang 1975)*

Frequency of force waves	Frequency of amplitude pulsation	F_f	F_b	Origins				
				$\Lambda(i_{st}=1, i_{rt}=1)$	$\Lambda(i_{ec, rt}=1)$	$\Lambda(i_{sa}=1)$	$\Lambda(i_{sa}=2)$	B_h
Hz	Hz							
				Speed = 2970 r/min				
1039	1.0	✓	✓	✓	✓			✓
1039	1.0	✓	✓	✓	✓	✓		✓
1089	1.0	✓	✓	✓	✓			✓
1139	1.0	✓	✓	✓	✓			✓
1139	1.0	✓	✓	✓	✓	✓		✓
1189	1.0	✓	✓	✓	✓			✓
1239	1.0	✓	✓	✓	✓	✓		✓
1239	1.0	✓	✓	✓	✓			✓
1239	1.0	✓	✓	✓	✓	✓	✓	✓
1339	1.0	✓	✓	✓	✓			✓
1339	1.0	✓	✓	✓	✓	✓	✓	✓
				Speed = 2700 r/min				
1040	10	✓	✓	✓	✓			✓
1040	10	✓	✓	✓	✓	✓		✓
1040	10	✓	✓	✓	✓		✓	✓
1085	10	✓	✓	✓	✓			✓
1085	10	✓	✓	✓	✓	✓		✓
1095	10	✓	✓	✓	✓	✓		✓
1095	10	✓	✓	✓	✓			✓
1140	10	✓	✓	✓	✓	✓		✓
1140	10	✓	✓	✓	✓			✓
1140	10	✓	✓	✓	✓		✓	✓

TABLE 3.3. *Continued*

Frequency of force waves	Frequency of amplitude pulsation	Origins						
		F_f	F_b	$\Lambda(i_{st}=1, i_{rt}=1)$	$\Lambda(i_{ec,\,rt}=1)$	$\Lambda(i_{sa}=1)$	$\Lambda(i_{sa}=2)$	B_h
				Speed = 2700 r/min				
1185	10	✓	✓	✓	✓			✓
1185	10	✓	✓	✓	✓	✓		✓
1230	10	✓	✓		✓			✓
1240	10	✓	✓	✓	✓		✓	✓

*Machine having 22 rotor and 12 stator slots.
Supply at 240 V and 50 Hz.
F_f = fundamental forward m.m.f.
F_b = fundamental backward m.m.f.
$\Lambda(i_{st}=1, i_{rt}=1)$ = fundamental stator/rotor slot permeance.
$\Lambda(i_{ec,\,rt}=1)$ = fundamental dynamic rotor-eccentricity permeance.
$\Lambda(i_{sa}=1)$ = fundamental iron-saturation permeance.
$\Lambda(i_{sa}=2)$ = 2nd harmonic iron-saturation permeance.
B_h = homopolar flux density waves.

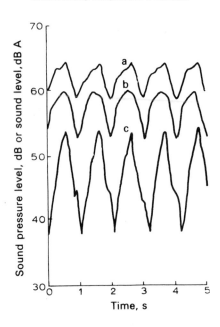

Fig. 3.3. Pulsating noise from a 2-pole motor in an anechoic chamber (Yang 1975). Speed = 2970 r/min

(a) In A weighting.
(b) In one-third octave band, centred at 1250 Hz.
(c) Narrow-band (1% of centre frequency) at 1239 Hz.

Apart from the first two terms in eqn (3.34), the rest of the equation represents the additional radial force waves related to the homopolar flux waves. The last term of eqn (3.34) gives a series of radial force waves having an amplitude pulsating at twice the slip frequency.

3.5. Effects of voltage/current harmonics

Many solid-state power-supply systems are used in variable speed drives. The voltage and current waveforms of these supply systems are often far from sinusoidal. This section will discuss the effects of voltage/current harmonics on radial force waves with special reference to a variable-speed 3-phase induction motor supplied from a variable-frequency inverter. The most significant voltage and current harmonics are usually the fifth, seventh and eleventh harmonics. Their amplitudes are quite often considerably higher than 10% of the fundamental. It is therefore necessary to consider these harmonics in analysing the magnetic force components. For clarity, taking into account only the m.m.f. waves due to the current harmonics up to the eleventh order and the space harmonics up to the fifth order and the fundamental stator/rotor slot permeance wave, the air gap flux density waves can be expressed as

TABLE 3.4. *Origin of zero-mode-number radial forces (Yang 1976)*

Frequency (Hz)	Origins*								
	F_{1-1}	F_{1-5}	F_{1-7}	F_{1-11}	F_{5-1}	F_{5-5}	F_{5-7}	F_{5-11}	$\Lambda_{i_{st}=1,\, i_{rt}=1}$
$6f_1$						√		√	√
$6f_1$	√	√							√
$6f_1$	√		√						√
$6f_1$		√		√					√
$6f_1$					√	√			√
$6f_1$					√		√		√
$12f_1$		√	√						√
$12f_1$	√			√					√
$12f_1$					√			√	√
$12f_1$						√	√		√
$18f_1$							√	√	√
$18f_1$		√	√						√

*F_{k-q} = m.m.f. due to the kth space harmonic and the qth current harmonic.
$\Lambda_{i_{st}=1,\, i_{rt}=1}$ = fundamental stator/rotor slot permeance.
f_1 = fundamental frequency.

$$B(\phi, t) = \Lambda_0 \{ F_{1-1} \cos(p\phi - \omega_1 t) + F_{5-1} \cos(5p\phi + \omega_1 t)$$
$$+ F_{1-5} \cos(p\phi + 5\omega_1 t) + F_{5-5} \cos(5p\phi - 5\omega_1 t)$$
$$+ F_{1-7} \cos(p\phi - 7\omega_1 t) + F_{5-7} \cos(5p\phi + 7\omega_1 t)$$
$$+ F_{1-11} \cos(p\phi + 11\omega_1 t) + F_{5-11} \cos(5p\phi - 11\omega_1 t) \}$$
$$+ \tfrac{1}{2} \Lambda_{i_{st}=1,\, i_{rt}=1} \left[\sum_{k,\,q} F_{k-q} \cos\{ (Z_{rt} \pm Z_{st} \pm kp)\phi - (Z_{rt}\omega_{rt} \pm q\omega_1)t \} \right]$$
$$(3.35)$$

where F_{k-q} represents the amplitude of the m.m.f. wave due to the kth space harmonic and the qth current harmonic.

Substituting the above expression in eqn (3.19) we have

$$\sigma_{ra}(\phi, t) = \sigma_{6\omega_1} \cos(6\omega_1 t) + \sigma_{12\omega_1} \cos(12\omega_1 t)$$
$$+ \sigma_{18\omega_1} \cos(18\omega_1 t) + \text{other terms.} \qquad (3.36)$$

The first three terms in eqn (3.36) are zero-mode-number force components and are produced by the interaction of two flux density wave components in eqn (3.35). For example, the interaction between $F_{1-1} \cos(p\phi - \omega_1 t)$ and $F_{1-5} \cos(p\phi + 5\omega_1 t)$ produced a zero-mode-number force at a frequency of $6\omega_1$. Many other combinations would also form forces at multiples of six times the fundamental frequency, ω_1. The origins of part of these zero-mode-number forces are shown in Table 3.4.

Table 3.4 shows that the interaction between the m.m.f. waves having the same space harmonic order but different current harmonic orders results in zero-

TABLE 3.5. *Characteristics of non-zero-mode-number radial forces (Yang 1976)*

Frequency (Hz)	Mode number of force wave	Origins*										
		F_{1-5}	F_{1-7}	F_{1-11}	F_{5-1}	F_{5-5}	F_{5-7}	F_{5-11}	F_{7-1}	F_{7-5}	F_{7-7}	F_{7-11}
$6f_1$	$6p$	✓			✓							
$6f_1$	$6p$	✓			✓				✓			
$6f_1$	$12p$				✓				✓	✓		
$6f_1$	$12p$				✓	✓			✓			
$6f_1$	$12p$						✓		✓✓		✓	
$6f_1$	$12p$				✓				✓			
$12f_1$	$6p$			✓								
$12f_1$	$12p$							✓✓				✓
$12f_1$	$12p$											
$18f_1$	$6p$		✓									

*F_{k-q} = m.m.f. due to the kth space harmonic and the qth current harmonic.
f_1 = fundamental frequency.
p = number of pole pairs.

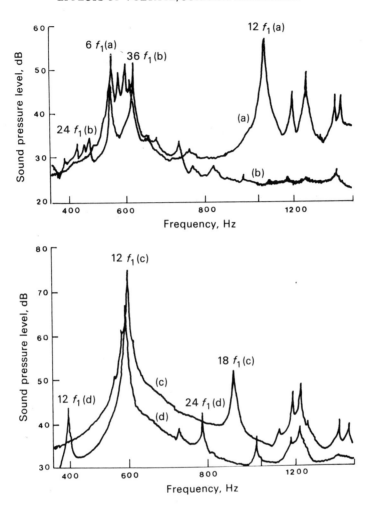

Fig. 3.4. Narrow-band noise spectra of a 3-phase 6-pole induction motor fed from an inverter (Yang 1976)

On no load
(a) $f_1 = 85.0\,\text{Hz}$ (b) $f_2 = 17.5\,\text{Hz}$
(c) $f_1 = 49.2\,\text{Hz}$ (d) $f_2 = 32.4\,\text{Hz}$

mode-number radial forces at frequencies of 6, 12, and 18 times the fundamental frequency. Furthermore, it can be shown that there are zero-mode-number forces at frequencies of $24\omega_1$, $30\omega_1$ and higher multiples of $6\omega_1$, if current harmonics of higher than eleventh order are taken into consideration. Based on eqns (3.35) and (3.19), and taking into account the space harmonics up to the seventh, it can be shown that there are a series of non-zero-mode-number force waves at frequencies of multiples of six times the fundamental frequency. The characteristics and origins of part of these waves are given in Table (3.5).

Table (3.5) shows that the interaction between the m.m.f. waves with different current and space harmonic orders produces a series of non-zero-mode-number force waves at multiples of six times the fundamental frequency. These force waves would reinforce those zero-mode-number forces at the same frequencies and could cause considerable noise and vibration, especially when these frequencies are near or equal to the natural frequencies of the machine structures. Fig. 3.4 gives an example (Yang 1976) of the noise spectra of a 3-phase motor supplied from an inverter and shows clearly that the predominant components are at multiples of six times the variable fundamental frequency.

Appendix 3.1

Derivation of eqns (3.29) and (3.33)

The fundamental forward and backward m.m.f. waves of a 2-pole single-phase induction machine are

$$F(\phi, t) = F_f \cos(\phi - \omega_1 t + \psi_f) + F_b \cos(\phi + \omega_1 t + \psi_b) \quad (A3.1)$$

where F_f and F_b are the amplitude of the forward and backward m.m.f. waves, respectively, and ψ_f and ψ_b are the phase angles.

The fundamental air-gap permeance wave due to static rotor eccentricity can be expressed by

$$\Lambda_1(\phi) = \Lambda_1 \cos(\phi + \psi_1') \quad (A3.2)$$

The product of the above two equations gives the following flux density waves in the air gap:

$$B_1(\phi, t) = \frac{\Lambda_1}{2} F_f \cos\{\omega_1 t + (\psi_1' - \psi_f)\} + \frac{\Lambda_1}{2} F_b \cos\{\omega_1 t + (\psi_b - \psi_1')\}$$

$$+ \frac{\Lambda_1 F_f}{2} \cos\{2\phi - \omega_1 t + (\psi_f + \psi_1')\}$$

$$+ \frac{\Lambda_1 F_b}{2} \cos\{2\phi + \omega_1 t + (\psi_b + \psi_1')\} \quad (A3.3)$$

The first two terms of the above expression represent homopolar flux waves at the supply frequency.

The fundamental air-gap permeance wave due to dynamic rotor eccentricity is given by (see eqn (3.7))

$$\Lambda_1'(\phi, t) = \Lambda_1' \cos(\phi - \omega_{ec} t + \psi_1'') \doteq \Lambda_1' \cos(\phi - \omega_{rt} t + \psi_1'') \quad (A3.4)$$

where ψ_1'' is the phase angle.

The product of eqns (A3.1) and (A3.4) produces the following flux density waves:

$$B_1'(\phi, t) = \frac{\Lambda_1'}{2} F_f \cos \{s\omega_1 t + (\psi_1'' - \psi_f)\}$$

$$+ \frac{\Lambda_1'}{2} F_b \cos \{(2 - s)\omega_1 t + (\psi_b - \psi_1'')\}$$

$$+ \frac{\Lambda_1'}{2} F_f \cos \{2\phi - (2 - s)\omega_1 t + (\psi_f + \psi_1'')\}$$

$$+ \frac{\Lambda_1'}{2} F_b \cos \{2\phi + s\omega_1 t + (\psi_b'' + \psi_1)\} \qquad (A3.5)$$

The first and second terms of the above expression represent two homopolar flux waves at frequencies of $s\omega_1$ and $(2 - s)\omega_1$, respectively.

The above derivation has not considered any reluctance in the flux paths except in the air gap. Since the homopolar flux waves have to complete their paths through the stator frame, the endshields, the bearings, the shaft and back to the stator and rotor cores, the magnitude of these homopolar waves also depends on the reluctance of these paths. Furthermore, there are magnetic permeance variations in core laminations (Yang 1975). The effects of these permeance variations on flux waves may, to a certain extent, be expressed as some equivalent air gap variation. Using a coefficient ϵ to take into account the effects of the additional reluctance in the homopolar flux paths and the equivalent air gap variations due to permeance variations, the homopolar flux waves in eqns (A3.3) and (A3.5) can be expressed as

$$B_h(t) = \epsilon \frac{\Lambda_1'}{2} F_f \cos (s\omega_1 t + \psi_1) + \epsilon' \frac{\Lambda_1'}{2} F_b \cos \{(2 - s)\omega_1 t + \psi_2\}$$

$$+ \epsilon'' \frac{\Lambda_1}{2} F_f \cos (\omega_1 t + \psi_3) + \epsilon'' \frac{\Lambda_1}{2} F_b \cos (\omega_1 t + \psi_4). \quad (A3.6)$$

Neglecting the phase angles, the above equation becomes eqn (3.29).

For a 2-pole 3-phase machine operating under balanced conditions, the fundamental m.m.f. wave is

$$F(\phi, t) = F_f \cos (\phi - \omega_1 t + \psi_f). \qquad (3.7)$$

Combining eqn (A3.7) with eqn (A3.2) and eqn (A3.4) and neglecting the phase angles, the homopolar flux waves are

$$B_h(t) = \epsilon \frac{\Lambda_1'}{2} F_f \cos (s\omega_1 t) + \epsilon'' \frac{\Lambda_1}{2} F_f \cos (\omega_1 t). \qquad (A3.8)$$

The above is eqn (3.33).

References

BINNS, K.J. (1968). Cogging torques in induction machines. *Proc. Instn elect. Engrs* **115**, 1783–90.

CHALMERS, B.J. (1965). *Electromagnetic problems of a.c. machines.* Chapman & Hall, London.

ELLISON, A.J. and YANG, S.J. (1971). Effects of rotor eccentricity on acoustic noise from induction machines. *Proc. Instn elect. Engrs* **118**, 174–84.

HARLIN, D. (1965). Oscillation behaviour in asynchronous motors as a result of unbalances. Dr. Ing. thesis, Stuttgart, Germany.

LIWSCHITZ-GARIK, M. and WHIPPLE, C.C. (1946). *Electric machinery.* D. Van Nostrand.

RANDELL, A.R. (1965). Performance of electric machines using a generalised theory and including air-gap flux harmonics. Ph.D. thesis, University of London.

SEELY, S. (1962). *Electromechanical energy conversion.* McGraw-Hill, New York.

YANG, S.J. (1975). Acoustic noise from small 2-pole single-phase induction machines. *Proc. Instn elect. Engrs* **122**, 1391–6.

———— (1976). Noise and vibration of inverter-fed induction motors. *Proc. Int. Conf. Electrical Machines,* Vienna, I9-1–I9-10.

4. Mechanical behaviour of stators

The magnetic force acting on the cores of the stator and rotor, and the mechanical vibratory forces acting on the bearings, may produce troublesome noise and vibration, especially when the frequencies of the exciting forces are equal or near to the natural frequencies of the machine concerned. Design engineers must be able to assess the natural frequencies of the stator and the rotor so that appropriate winding or structural designs can be arranged to give a mismatch of the frequencies of the important exciting force waves and the natural frequencies of the machine.

As far as the production of direct airborne noise is concerned, the radial vibration of the stator structure is, in most practical cases, the predominant noise source. The following will therefore concentrate on stator radial vibrations.

4.1. Stator radial vibration modes

In general, the stator radial vibration along its circumference can be expressed as

$$A_{rd} = \sum_{i=0}^{\infty} A_{rd, \, m_i, \, \omega_i} \cos \left(m_i \phi + \omega_i t + \psi_{m_i, \, \omega_i} \right) \qquad (4.1)$$

where m is the circumferential mode of vibration, ϕ is the angular position, ω is the angular frequency and ψ is the phase angle. Fig. 4.1 shows the shapes of the stator radial deflections for $m = 0-5$.

From airborne noise point of view, the most important circumferential modes of vibration for small machines are 1, 2, 3, and 4. However, higher modes may become important for medium-sized and large machines. In many cases, $m = 2$ is the most predominant mode. However, $m = 1$ may become predominant if there is a one-pole-pair force wave with a frequency equal or near to the rotor critical speed (Saito and Maeda 1971).

Owing to radial force waves rotating in both clockwise and anti-clockwise directions, standing wave radial vibration patterns are often formed along the circumference of the stator surface. Fig. 4.2 shows one of the examples for the standing wave vibration pattern.

Along a generatrix on the stator surface, the radial vibration level is usually not constant. In general, it may take various forms, as shown in Fig. 4.3. In practice, except for very long stator structures, the most important longitudinal mode of vibration is that having a longitudinal mode number of 0.

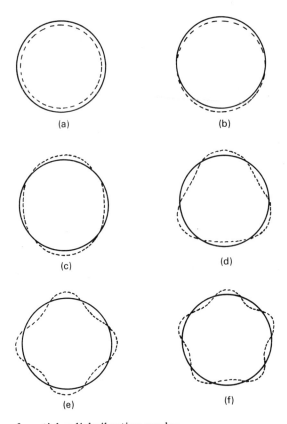

Fig. 4.1. Circumferential radial vibration modes

(a) $m = 0$ (b) $m = 1$ (c) $m = 2$
(d) $m = 3$ (e) $m = 4$ (f) $m = 5$

4.2. Natural frequencies of stators

Den Hartog (1928) studied a method for calculating the natural frequencies of a stator of the single-ring type in 1928. Later, Jordan (1957), Frohne (1959) and Üner (1964) introduced the effects of shear, rotary inertia, teeth, and winding into the calculation. Voronetskii (1956) and Lübcke (1956) presented methods that added experimentally determined factors to the classic formula. Pavlovsky (1968) treated the stator as a single thick ring loaded with teeth and winding and derived numerical tables calculating the stator natural frequencies. Recently, Holzmann (1970) studied the effects of tooth potential energy on stator natural frequencies. Verma and Girgis (1974) investigated the effects of core thickness and core lengths. Nevertheless, the effect of stator winding on natural frequencies is not yet fully understood and none of the methods available gives very accurate results.

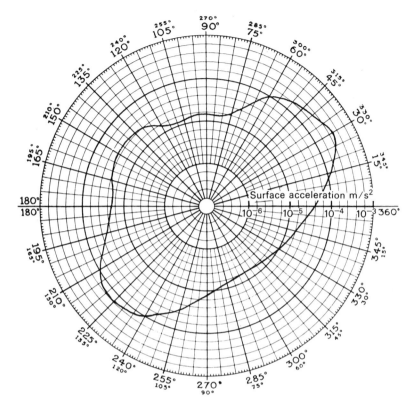

Fig. 4.2. Example of standing wave vibration pattern on a 75 W motor surface
(narrow-band frequency = 1000 Hz)

4.2.1. Single-ring type

To estimate the approximate natural frequency value, the following simple
formulae derived by Jordan, Frohne and Üner (Jordan and Frohne 1957; Frohne
1959; Üner and Jordan 1964), taking into account the effects of shear, rotary
inertia, teeth, and winding can be used.

4.2.1.1. Pulsating vibration mode

The pulsating vibration mode is shown in Fig. 4.1(a), i.e. $m = 0$. The natural
frequency is given by

$$f_{m=0} = \frac{1}{2\pi R_{\mathrm{m}}} \left(\frac{E}{\rho\Delta}\right)^{1/2} \tag{4.2}$$

where E is the modulus of elasticity of the core material (kgf/cm^2), R_{m} is the
mean radius (cm) excluding teeth (see Fig. 4.4), ρ is the density of the core

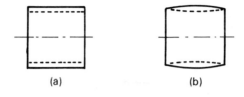

Fig. 4.3. Longitudinal radial vibration modes

(a) $n = 0$ (c) $n = 2$
(b) $n = 1$ (d) $n = 3$

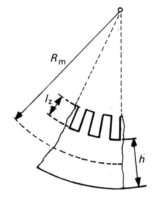

Fig. 4.4. Part of a single-ring stator structure

R_m Mean radius
h Core thickness
l_z Tooth height

material (kg/cm³), i.e. in kgf-s²/cm⁴, and Δ is the mass addition factor for displacement which is defined as

$$\Delta = 1 + \frac{G_z + G_W + G_B}{G_j} \qquad (4.3)$$

Where G_z is the total weight of the teeth, G_W is the winding weight, G_B is the weight of insulation, and G_j is the stator yoke weight, i.e. the weight of stator core without teeth, winding, and insulation.

4.2.1.2. Unity circumferential vibration mode

The unity circumferential vibration mode is shown in Fig. 4.1(b), i.e. $m = 1$. The approximate natural frequency is given by

$$f_{m=1} = f_{m=0} \left(\frac{2}{1 + i^2 \frac{\Delta_m}{\Delta}} \right)^{1/2} \tag{4.4}$$

where $f_{m=0}$ is the pulsating mode natural frequency determined by eqn (4.2), Δ is defined by eqn (4.3), i is defined as

$$i = \frac{1}{2\sqrt{3}} \frac{h}{R_m} \tag{4.5}$$

where h is the thickness of the core (cm), see Fig. 4.4, and Δ_m is the mass addition factor for rotation and is defined as

$$\Delta_m = 1 + \frac{Z_{st}\theta_z}{2\pi I R_m} \tag{4.6}$$

where Z_{st} is the stator slot number, $I = bh^3/12$, where b is the stator core length (cm), h is the core thickness (cm), θ_z is defined as

$$\theta_z = F_z^* l_z^3 \left\{ \frac{1}{3} + \left(\frac{h}{2l_z}\right) + \left(\frac{h}{2l_z}\right)^2 \right\} \tag{4.7}$$

where l_z is the tooth height (cm) (see Fig. 4.4), and F_z^* is given by

$$F_z^* = F_z \frac{G_z + G_W + G_B}{G_z} \tag{4.8}$$

where F_z is the mean tooth cross sectional area (cm^2), and G_z, G_W, and G_B have the same meaning as in eqn (4.3).

4.2.1.3. Circumferential vibration modes $\geqslant 2$

For any circumferential vibration mode greater than or equal to two, the approximate frequency is given by

$$f_{m \geqslant 2} = \frac{f_{m=0} \, im(m^2 - 1)\phi_m}{\sqrt{(m^2 + 1)}} \tag{4.9}$$

where $f_{m=0}$ is determined by eqn (4.2), i is defined by eqn (4.5), m is the mode number, and ϕ_m is given by

$$\phi_m = \left\{ 1 + \frac{i^2(m^2 - 1)\left(m^2\left(4 + \frac{\Delta_m}{\Delta}\right) + 3\right)}{m^2 + 1} \right\}^{-1/2} . \qquad (4.10)$$

From the viewpoint of noise emission, the most important vibration mode is $m = 2$. Substituting $m = 2$ into eqns (4.9) and (4.10)

$$f_{m=2} = \frac{2.685 i f_{m=0}}{\left\{ 1 + 0.6 i^2 \left(19 + 4\frac{\Delta_m}{\Delta} \right) \right\}^{1/2}} . \qquad (4.11)$$

4.2.2. Double-ring type

Many stators of electric machines are of double-ring type, consisting of an outer frame and an inner stator core. The frame is linked to the core laminations by ribs or key bars. Assuming the structure to be two thin rings joined by key bars, Erdelyi (1955) developed a method to calculate the stator natural frequencies of a medium-sized induction motor. However, for special low noise machines, small machines and 2-pole medium-sized machines, the ratio of the thickness of the core laminations to the mean radius of the core may well exceed 0.2. Therefore the assumption of two thin rings may lead to inaccurate and unsatisfactory results. Ellison and Yang (1971) investigated the natural frequencies of a stator consisting of a thin frame and a thick core loaded with teeth and windings and solidly coupled at key bars, taking into account shear, extension, and rotary inertia. The details of their method are described in the reference and a brief summary of the major steps is given below.

(a) To calculate the kinetic energy of the whole system: the radial displacement of the frame and core can be assumed as

$$u = \sum_{m=1}^{\infty} (a_m \cos m\theta + b_m \sin m\theta) \qquad (4.12)$$

Where the coefficients a_m and b_m are time functions and each of the coefficients can be expressed as the product of a numerical amplitude and $e^{j\omega t}$. These coefficients are called the generalized co-ordinates of the system. The kinetic energy of the system can be expressed in terms of the generalized co-ordinates, the machine dimensions, and the material constants.

(b) To calculate the potential energy of the whole system: the potential energy can also be expressed in terms of the generalized co-ordinates, the machine dimensions, and the material constants.

(c) To derive a set of equations of motion for the system by using the following Lagrange's equation:

$$\frac{\partial}{\partial t} \left(\frac{\partial L}{\partial \dot{x}_m} \right) - \frac{\partial L}{\partial x_m} = 0 \qquad (4.13)$$

where x_m is one of the generalized co-ordinates, L is the difference between the total kinetic energy of the system, T_{tot}, and the total potential energy of the system, U_{tot}. The set of equations can be written in matrix form as

$$[A] \ [X] - \omega^2 [M] \ [X] = 0 \qquad (4.14)$$

where $[A]$ is a symmetric matrix and $[M]$ is a diagonal matrix.
(d) To solve eqn (4.14): eqn (4.14) has a non-zero solution if and only if the determinant of the coefficient matrix vanishes, i.e.

$$|[A] - \omega^2 [M]| = 0 \qquad (4.15)$$

From the roots of eqn (4.15), the natural frequencies of the system and the vibration modes can be found.

4.2.3. Asymmetrical type

In Sections 4.2.1 and 4.2.2, we assumed the machine stator structure to be a uniform cylindrical structure, the effects of the air-duct spacers, connecting box, non-uniform stator core thickness, and other irregularities being neglected. Therefore, these methods cannot give accurate natural frequency results for those stators having significant non-uniform or irregular structures. As expected, Hübner (1971) found experimentally that the number and location of the air-duct spacers considerably affected the stator natural frequencies. In order to take into account all detailed structure dimensions, Thomson (1977) tried the finite difference method to calculate small motor stator natural frequencies but found that the accuracy was limited by the difficulty in simulating sharp boundary changes. Shumilov (1974) suggested the use of the finite element method for stator vibration analysis but gave no concrete results on any machine model. Yang (1978) tested the finite element method on d.c. machine stator models (see Tables 4.1 and 4.2). Tables 4.1 and 4.2 show that the finite element method gives more accurate results in comparison with Holtzmann's energy method (1970). The accuracy of the finite element method can be further improved by increasing the number of elements used in the analysis or by using high-order elements with the penalty of increased computing cost. The main advantage of the finite element method is that it can take into account the detailed dimensions of the stator structure, e.g. non-uniform pole and slot dimensions and other irregularities, since the elements can be graded in shape and size to follow arbitrary boundaries. The details of the finite element method can be found in Zienkiewicz and Cheung (1967).

TABLE 4.1. *Natural frequencies of Model 1 (Yang 1978)*

Vibration mode m / Natural frequency	Measured values f_{mea} (Hz)	By finite-element analysis with 80 elements		By Holzmann's method	
		f_{cal} (Hz)	Error (%)	f_{cal} (Hz)	Error (%)
3	902	925	+2.5	834	−7.4
5	2374	2177	−8.3	2078	−12.4
7	3310	3297	−0.3	3530	+6.6

TABLE 4.2. *Natural frequencies of Model 2 (Yang 1978)*

Vibration mode m / Natural frequency	Measured values f_{mea} (Hz)	By finite-element analysis with 72 elements		By Holzmann's method	
		f_{cal} (Hz)	Error (%)	f_{cal} (Hz)	Error (%)
3	984	1007	+2.3	900	−8.5
4	2082	2052	−4.1	1685	−19.1
5	2920	2936	+0.5	2201	−24.6
6	3350	3510	+4.8	3044	−9.1

4.3. Damping characteristics and stator deflections

Damping means the ability of the structure to absorb vibrational energy due to internal friction. When an exciting force is equal or close to one of the natural frequencies of a structure, the amplitude of vibration is determined by the damping capacity of the structure. It is quite often the case that one or more of the natural frequencies of the machine is not far away from the frequencies of a periodic exciting force. Under these circumstances, it is necessary to consider the damping in calculating the amplitude of vibration.

One of the common parameters to describe the damping property is the logarithmic decrement, δ. For low damping and at steady-state resonance, the logarithmic decrement can be determined from a resonance curve by the following expression (Fiore and Brach 1969):

$$\delta = \frac{\pi \Delta f}{f_{res}} \tag{4.16}$$

where f_{res} is the resonance frequency and Δf is the width (Hz) of the resonance peak at which the amplitude of vibration is 0.707 times that at resonance. The surface vibrations should be measured when the exciting external force acting on the stator structure is kept constant. The external force can be checked with a force gauge. By varying the frequency of the excitation force, a resonance curve

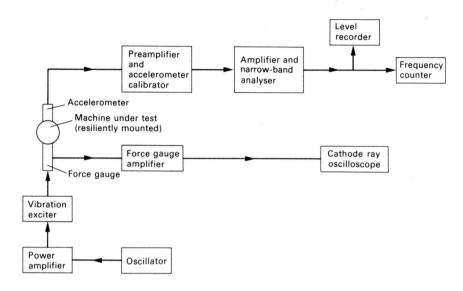

Fig. 4.5. Arrangements of apparatus for resonance tests on electric motors

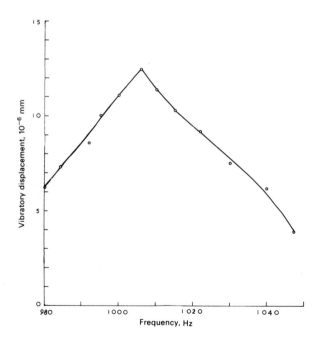

Fig. 4.6. Example of resonance curve for a 7.5 kW motor

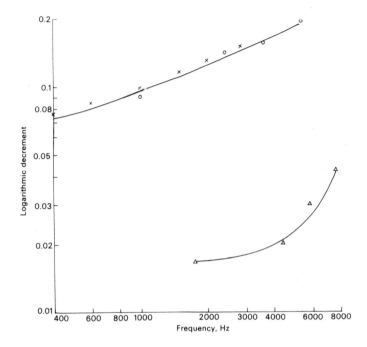

Fig. 4.7. Variation of logarithmic decrement with frequency (Yang 1970)

○　Yang's data
×　Hübner's data
△　Stator core without winding

and hence the corresponding logarithmic decrement can be obtained. Fig. 4.5 shows the test arrangement and Fig. 4.6 shows an example of the resonance curve obtained from a small machine. The results for δ values obtained by Yang (1970) and Hübner (1959) for small and medium sized machines are shown in Fig. 4.7. Although the results were taken at several discrete frequencies, Fig. 4.7 shows that there is a tendency for the logarithmic decrements to increase gradually with frequency. Yang also tested a stator core without a winding and its logarithmic decrements were found to be much lower than those carrying windings (see Fig. 4.7). This difference is most likely caused by the additional energy dissipation in winding-to-core friction and in the windings themselves. Girgis and Verma (1979) found that the damping of the laminated stator structure was significantly greater than that of a solid steel structure.

For a large turbogenerator, Borderl et al. (Börderl, Jordan and Röder 1967) found that the damping factor, D, at a frequency near 100 Hz was 0.063. Since logarithmic decrement is equal to $2\pi D$, the logarithmic decrement is approximately equal to 0.4 for the turbogenerator.

For vibration modes $m \geqslant 2$, the static radial deflection of the stator core can

can be determined by

$$(A_{\mathrm{rd}})_{\mathrm{static}} = \frac{12\hat{\sigma}_{\mathrm{ra}}R_{\mathrm{m}}}{m^4 E}\left(\frac{R_{\mathrm{m}}}{h}\right)^3 \qquad (4.17)$$

where A_{rd} is the amplitude of static deflection (cm), $\hat{\sigma}_{\mathrm{ra}}$ is the amplitude of the radial force wave (N/cm^2), R_{m} is the mean radius and h is the stator core thickness (cm), excluding teeth, (see Fig. 4.4) and E is the core material modulus of elasticity (N/cm^2).

Considering the damping and resonance effects, the dynamic radial deflection of the stator core can be expressed by

$$R_{\mathrm{rd, dyn}} = A_{\mathrm{rd, static}}\left[\left\{1 - \left(\frac{f_{\mathrm{exc}}}{f_{\mathrm{res}}}\right)^2\right\}^2 + \left(\frac{\delta}{\pi}\frac{f_{\mathrm{exc}}}{f_{\mathrm{res}}}\right)^2\right]^{-1/2} \qquad (4.18)$$

where f_{res} is the natural frequency of a particular mode and f_{exc} is the exciting force frequency of the given mode.

Eqns (4.17) and (4.18) give only approximate results since eqn (4.17) implicitly assumes:

(a) the stiffening effects of the stator teeth and frame are negligible

(b) the deflection is the same as that of a uniform beam freely supported at both ends with a sinusoidally distributed load.

Neglecting the effect of teeth, Kerruish (1958) derived an accurate expression to calculate the deflection of a smooth thick ring structure when subjected to a sinusoidally distributed load on its inner surface. For a 2-pole-pair exciting force wave, i.e. for a vibration mode of $m = 2$, the amplitude of the static deflection on the outer surface is given by

$$(A_{\mathrm{rd}})_{\mathrm{static},\, m=2} = \frac{\hat{\sigma}_{\mathrm{ra}}b}{6E\left(\frac{b^2}{a^2} - 1\right)^3}\left\{24\left(\frac{b^2}{a^2}\right)^2 + 16\left(\frac{b}{a}\right)^2 + 24\right\} \qquad (4.19)$$

where b and a are the outer and inner radius, respectively, and $\hat{\sigma}_{\mathrm{ra}}$ and E have the same meaning as in eqn (4.17). For accurate deflection values, it is necessary to use the finite element method (Zienkiewicz and Cheung 1967), taking into account the effects of teeth and frame.

References

BÖRDERL, P., JORDAN, H. and RÖDER, G. (1967). Ermittlung der Biegeeigenfrequenz für die Vierknotenschwingung des Ständerbleckpakets von Turbogeneratoren. *AEG Mitt.* **57**, 35–9.

DEN HARTOG, J.P. (1928). Vibration of frames of electrical machines. *Trans. am. Soc. mech. Engrs* **50**, 1–6 and 9–11.

ELLISON, A.J. and YANG, S.J. (1971). Natural frequencies of stators of small electric machines. *Proc. Instn elect. Engrs* 118, 185–90.
ERDELYI, E. (1955). Predetermination of the sound pressure levels of magnetic noise in medium induction motors. Ph.D. thesis, University of Michigan.
FIORE, N.F. and BRACH, R.M. (1969). Resonance-bar damping measurements by the resonance buildup technique. *J. acoust. Soc. Am.*, 46, 492–5.
FROHNE, H. (1959). Über die primaren Bestismmungsgrössen der Lautstärke bei Asynchronmaschinen. Dr. Ing. thesis, Technical University of Hanover.
GIRGIS, R.S. and VERMA, S.P. (1979). Resonant frequencies and vibration behaviour of stators of electrical machines as affected by teeth, windings, frame and laminations. *IEEE Trans. Power Appar. Syst.* PAS–98, 1446–55.
HOLZMANN, F. (1970). Swingungsberechnung fur Modelle von Gehausen Elektrischer Maschinen mit Hilfe der Energie methode. Dr. Ing. thesis, T.U. Braunschweig.
HÜBNER, G. (1959). Uber das Schwingungserhalten von Wechselstrommaschinen-Standern mit Rundschnitt-Blechpaketen. *Elektrotech. Z. ETZA*, 80, 33–9.
HÜBNER, G.H. and SEHRNDT, G.A. (1971). Zur Berechnung Magnetisch verursachter Gerausche Rotierender Elektrischer Maschinen-Schwingungs-verhalten Segmentierter Blechpakete. *Proc. 7th Int. Congr. Acoustics*, Budapest, 709–12.
JORDAN, H. and FROHNE, H. (1957). Ermittlung der Eigenfrequenzen des Ständers von Drehstrommotoren. *Lärmbekämpfung*, 7, 137–40.
KERRUISH, N. (1958). Deflexion of a thick cylindrical ring due to a sinusoidal force. *Elect. Energy*, 2, 236–8.
LÜBCKE, E. (1956). Korperschallprobleme in Elektromaschinenbau. *VDI-Ber.*, 8, 65–70.
PAVLOVSKY, H. (1968). Vypocet vlastnich kmitoctu statorovych, svazku elektrickych stroju, Elektrickych stroju. *Elektrotech. Obz.* 57, 305–11.
SAITO, F. and MAEDA, S. (1971). Experimental investigation of magnetic noise in polyphase induction motors. National Technical Report (Japan), 17, 341–9.
SHUMILOV, J.A. (1974). Calculating stator vibrations in electrical machines, *Proc. Int. Conf. Electrical Machines*, London.
THOMSON, W.T. (1977). Vibration and noise in small-power electric motors. M.Sc. thesis, Strathclyde University.
ÜNER, Z. and JORDAN, H. (1964). Berechnung der Eigenfrequenzen der Blechpakete von Drehstrommaschinen. *Konstruktion* 16, 108–11.
VERMA, S.P. and GIRGIS, R.S. (1974). Considerations in the choice of main dimensions of stators of electrical machines in relation to their vibration characteristics. IEEE Industry Applications Society Meeting, Pittsburgh.
VORONETSKII, B.B. (1956). Natural frequencies of a.c. electrical machine stators. *Vest. Elektromprom.* 7, 52–7.
YANG, S.J. (1970). The measurement and calculation of acoustic noise from electric machines. Ph.D. thesis, University of London.
——— (1978). Finite element method in evaluating the stator natural frequencies of small machines. *Proc. Int. Conf. Electrical Machines*, Brussels.
ZIENKIEWICZ, O.C. and CHEUNG, Y.K. (1967). *The finite element method in structural and continuum mechanics.* McGraw-Hill, New York.

5. Sound radiation due to magnetic forces

5.1. Introduction

The surfaces of many electric machines are basically of cylindrical form and the surface vibration due to magnetic force waves may be regarded as a series of rotating sinusoidal waves of displacement. For calculating the sound intensity around a machine, Alger (1965) treated the machine as an infinitely long cylinder. This will give satisfactory results only for the middle part of a long machine. Carter (1932) assumed the machine to be a spherical source, but his solution for the sound power contains an undetermined constant and cannot be used in quantitative calculations. Jordan (1949) considered the stator core of a machine as an approximation to a sphere and has derived a method for calculating the sound intensity at the machine surface.

Erdelyi (1955) considered the machine as an infinitely long cylinder with travelling waves of vibration in a band corresponding to the length of the stator. His method is appropriate for electric machines with predominant magnetic noise in which only the sound pressure in a place passing through the centre and perpendicular to the shaft of the machine is required. Erdelyi did not study the variation of sound pressure along the axial direction nor a method of calculating the total sound power. Ellison and Moore (1969) presented a method for calculating sound power radiated from a short machine which has its diameter approximately equal to its length.

The following sections describe studies of the calculation of the total sound power produced by the surface vibrations of electric machines but without the limitation of a unity length–diameter ratio.

5.2. The sound pressure around an electric machine

In the following analysis, the surface of the machine is assumed to be a smooth cylindrical surface and the effects of connecting boxes, mounting device and endshields are ignored. For this simplified surface it is appropriate to use cylindrical co-ordinates. The co-ordinate system, in conjunction with the simplified machine surface, is shown in Fig. 5.1.

The wave equation for pressure p, in three dimensions and in a homogeneous medium, is given by (Rschevkin, 1963)

$$\nabla^2 p = \frac{1}{c^2} \frac{\partial^2 p}{\partial t^2} \qquad (5.1)$$

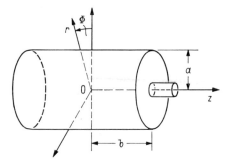

Fig. 5.1. Co-ordinate system and simplified machine surface

where ∇^2 is the Laplacian operator, c is the speed of sound and t is time. Assuming the pressure variation to be one of simple harmonic time dependence, the above equation becomes

$$(\nabla^2 + k^2)p = 0 \qquad (5.2)$$

where $k = \omega/c$ and ω is the angular frequency. In cylindrical co-ordinates, eqn (5.2) can be written as

$$\frac{1}{r}\left[\frac{\partial}{\partial r}\left\{r\left(\frac{\partial p}{\partial r}\right)\right\}\right] + \frac{1}{r^2}\left(\frac{\partial^2 p}{\partial \phi^2}\right) + \frac{\partial^2 p}{\partial z^2} + k^2 p = 0 \qquad (5.3)$$

where r is the radius, ϕ the angular position and z the axial distance from the centre of the machine (see Fig. 5.1).

Let the pressure be assumed to be as the following:

$$p(r, \phi, z) = Z(z)\Phi(\phi)R(r). \qquad (5.4)$$

Combining eqns (5.3) and (5.4) the following equations are obtained:

$$Z(z) = e^{jhz} + e^{-jhz} \qquad (5.5)$$

$$\Phi(\phi) = e^{jn\phi} + e^{-jn\phi} \qquad (5.6)$$

$$R(r) = A_r J_n\{r\sqrt{(k^2 - h^2)}\} + B_r Y_n\{r\sqrt{(k^2 - h^2)}\} \qquad (5.7)$$

where J_n and Y_n are Bessel functions of the 1st kind and 2nd kind, respectively, A_r, B_r, and h are constants and n is an integer.

Thus the general solution expressing the pressure is given by

$$p(r, \phi, z, t) = [A_r J_n\{r\sqrt{(k^2 - h^2)}\} + B_r Y_n\{r\sqrt{(k^2 - h^2)}\}]$$
$$(e^{jn\phi} + e^{-jn\phi})(e^{jhz} + e^{-jhz})e^{-j\omega t} \qquad (5.8)$$

The above equation provides an infinite number of solutions and the particular solution which determines the field around an electric machine can be found by the boundary conditions given by the surface vibration of the machine.

For an outgoing wave produced by a travelling vibration wave on the surface with a single mode number m, and assuming the amplitude of vibration along a generatrix of the stator surface to be constant, the surface vibratory displacement can be expressed as

$$A_{rd}(\phi, t) = A_{rd} e^{j(m\phi - \omega t)} \qquad (5.9)$$

for $-b < z < +b$ and the particular solution for the pressure is found to be (Ellison and Yang 1971)

$$p_i(r, \phi, z, t) = \frac{A_{rd}\omega^2 \rho b}{\pi}$$

$$e^{j(m\phi - \omega t)} \left[\int_{-k+\epsilon}^{k-\epsilon} \frac{2 \sin (bh)}{bh\sqrt{(k^2 - h^2)}} \left\{ \frac{Q_A Q_C + Q_B Q_D}{Q_C^2 + Q_D^2} + j \frac{Q_B Q_C - Q_A Q_D}{Q_C^2 + Q_D^2} \right\} dh \right.$$

$$\left. -4 \int_{0+\epsilon}^{\infty} \cos \left\{ \sqrt{\left(k^2 + \frac{\chi^2}{a^2}\right)} z \right\} \frac{\sin\left\{\frac{b}{a}\sqrt{(a^2 k^2 + \chi^2)}\right\}}{\frac{b}{a} (a^2 k^2 + \chi^2)} \cdot \frac{K_m\left(\frac{r}{a}\chi\right)}{K_{m-1}(\chi) + K_{m+1}(\chi)} d\chi \right]$$

$$(5.10)$$

where

$$Q_A = \cos (hz) J_m \{r\sqrt{(k^2 - h^2)}\} - \sin (hz) Y_m \{r\sqrt{(k^2 - h^2)}\}$$

$$Q_B = \cos (hz) Y_m \{r\sqrt{(k^2 - h^2)}\} + \sin (hz) J_m \{r\sqrt{(k^2 - h^2)}\}$$

$$Q_C = J_{m-1}\{a\sqrt{(k^2 - h^2)}\} - J_{m+1}\{a\sqrt{(k^2 - h^2)}\}$$

$$Q_D = Y_{m-1}\{a\sqrt{(k^2 - h^2)}\} - Y_{m+1}\{a\sqrt{(k^2 - h^2)}\}$$

$$\chi = -j\{a\sqrt{(k^2 - h^2)}\}$$

and K_i is the modified Bessel function (as defined in Abramowitz and Stegun 1965, p. 375), J_i is the Bessel function of the first kind and Y_i is the Bessel function of the second kind. Thus the sound pressure around the cylindrical surface for any value of z (for $r \geqslant a$) is determined.

The r.m.s. value of sound pressure around the machine is then found as

$$p = \frac{A_{rd}\omega^2 b\rho}{\sqrt{2\pi}} (Q_{PR}^2 + Q_{PM}^2)^{1/2} \qquad (5.11)$$

where

$$Q_{\mathrm{pR}} = \int_{-k+\epsilon}^{k-\epsilon} \frac{2 \sin (bh)}{bh\sqrt{(k^2 - h^2)}} \left(\frac{Q_A Q_C + Q_B Q_D}{Q_C^2 + Q_D^2} \right) dh$$

$$-4 \int_{0+\epsilon}^{\infty} \cos \left\{ \sqrt{\left(k^2 + \frac{\chi^2}{a^2}\right)} z \right\} \frac{\sin \left\{ \frac{b}{a} \sqrt{(a^2 k^2 + \chi^2)} \right\}}{\frac{b}{a} (a^2 k^2 + \chi^2)} \frac{K_m \left(\frac{r}{a} \chi \right)}{K_{m-1}(\chi) + K_{m+1}(\chi)} d\chi$$

and

$$Q_{\mathrm{pM}} = \int_{-k+\epsilon}^{k-\epsilon} \frac{2 \sin (bh)}{bh\sqrt{(k^2 - h^2)}} \left(\frac{Q_B Q_C - Q_A Q_D}{Q_C^2 + Q_D^2} \right) dh.$$

5.3. The particle velocity

The calculation of particle velocity is useful as one can then check analytically whether or not a particular point in the noise field is in the far field where both sound pressure and particle velocity are almost in phase. Furthermore, if the general expressions for sound pressure and particle velocity are known, it becomes possible to calculate the sound power from (Rschevkin 1963)

$$P = \int_A \tfrac{1}{2} \operatorname{Re} \{p_i(t) v_i^*(t)\} \, dA \tag{5.12}$$

where $v_i^*(t)$ means the conjugate of velocity $v_i(t)$ and A is the total surface area enclosing the machine. It should be emphasized that the surface A in eqn (5.12) could be any convenient one even very close to the surface of the machine as $p_i v_i^*$ has taken into account the phase difference between sound pressure and particle velocity. From Newton's Law, the velocity perpendicular to the cylindrical surface is (Rschevkin 1963)

$$v_i(r, \phi, z, t) = \frac{1}{j\omega\rho} \frac{\partial p(r, \phi, z, t)}{\partial r} \tag{5.13}$$

Combining eqns (5.10) and (5.13), the radial velocity is found as

$$v_i(r, \phi, z, t) = \frac{A_{\mathrm{rd}} \omega b}{\pi} e^{j(m\phi - \omega t - \pi/2)} \left[\int_{-k+\epsilon}^{k-\epsilon} \frac{2 \sin (bh)}{bh\sqrt{(k^2 - h^2)}} \frac{\xi_A Q_C + \xi_B Q_D}{Q_C^2 + Q_D^2} dh \right.$$

$$\left. + \int_{0+\epsilon}^{\infty} \frac{2\chi}{a} \cos \left\{ \sqrt{\left(k^2 + \frac{\chi^2}{a^2}\right)} z \right\} \frac{\sin \left\{ \frac{b}{a} \sqrt{(a^2 k^2 + \chi^2)} \right\}}{\frac{b}{a} (a^2 k^2 + \chi^2)} \times \right.$$

$$\left. \frac{K_{m-1}\left(\frac{r}{a}\chi\right) + K_{m+1}\left(\frac{r}{a}\chi\right)}{K_{m-1}(\chi) + K_{m+1}(\chi)} d\chi + j\int_{-k+\epsilon}^{k-\epsilon} \frac{2\sin(bh)}{bh\sqrt{(k^2-h^2)}}\frac{\xi_B Q_C - \xi_A Q_D}{Q_C^2 + Q_D^2} dh \right]$$

$$(5.14)$$

where

$$\xi_A = \sqrt{(k^2-k^2)}\cos(hz)\left[J_{m-1}\{r\sqrt{(k^2-h^2)}\}\right.$$

$$\left. -\frac{m}{r\sqrt{(k^2-h^2)}}J_m\{r\sqrt{(k^2-h^2)}\}\right]$$

$$-\sqrt{(k^2-h^2)}\sin(hz)\left[Y_{m-1}\{r\sqrt{(k^2-h^2)}\}\right.$$

$$\left. -\frac{m}{r\sqrt{(k^2-h^2)}}Y_m\{r\sqrt{(k^2-h^2)}\}\right]$$

and

$$\xi_B = \sqrt{(k^2-h^2)}\cos(hz)\left[Y_{m-1}\{r\sqrt{(k^2-h^2)}\}\right.$$

$$\left. -\frac{m}{r\sqrt{(k^2-h^2)}}Y_m\{r\sqrt{(k^2-h^2)}\}\right]$$

$$+\sqrt{(k^2-h^2)}\sin(hz)\left[J_{m-1}\{r\sqrt{(k^2-h^2)}\}\right.$$

$$\left. -\frac{m}{r\sqrt{(k^2-h^2)}}J_m\{r\sqrt{(k^2-h^2)}\}\right]$$

The r.m.s. value of velocity is given by

$$v = \frac{A_{rd}\omega b}{\sqrt{2\pi}}(Q_{vR}^2 + Q_{vM}^2)^{1/2} \qquad (5.15)$$

where

$$Q_{vR} = \int_{-k+\epsilon}^{k-\epsilon} \frac{2\sin(bh)}{bh\sqrt{(k^2-h^2)}}\frac{\xi_A Q_C + \xi_B Q_D}{Q_C^2 + Q_D^2} dh$$

$$+ \int_{0+\epsilon}^{\infty} \frac{2\chi}{a}\cos\left\{\sqrt{\left(k^2+\frac{\chi^2}{a^2}\right)}z\right\} \frac{\sin\left\{\frac{b}{a}\sqrt{(a^2k^2+\chi^2)}\right\}}{\frac{b}{a}(a^2k^2+\chi^2)} \times$$

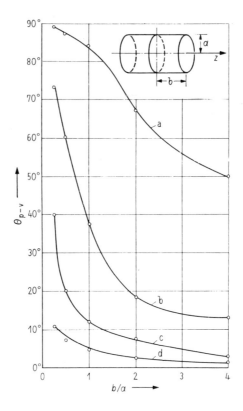

Fig. 5.2. Variation of phase difference between pressure and velocity $\theta_{p\text{-}v}$, with length–diameter ratio b/a ($a = 0.5$ m, $z = 0$, $m = 2$, $r = 1.5$ m) (Ellison and Yang 1971)

(a) $kr = 1.72$ (b) $kr = 3.44$

(c) $kr = 6.88$ (d) $kr = 27.56$

$$\frac{K_{m-1}\left(\frac{r}{a}\chi\right) + K_{m+1}\left(\frac{r}{a}\chi\right)}{K_{m-1}(\chi) + K_{m+1}(\chi)}\, d\chi$$

and

$$Q_{vM} = \int_{-k+\epsilon}^{k-\epsilon} \frac{2\sin(bh)}{bh\sqrt{(k^2 - h^2)}} \frac{\xi_B Q_C - \xi_A Q_D}{Q_C^2 + Q_D^2}\, dh.$$

The phase angle between the sound pressure and the particle velocity is found as

$$\theta_{p\text{-}v} = \frac{\pi}{2} + \tan^{-1}(Q_{pM}/Q_{pR}) - \tan^{-1}(Q_{vM}/Q_{vR}). \tag{5.16}$$

The above equation shows that the phase angle between sound pressure and

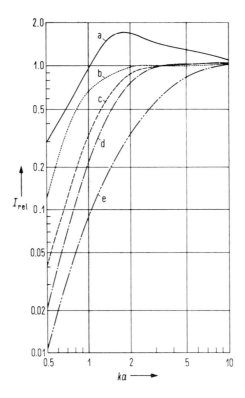

Fig. 5.3. Variation of relative sound intensity coefficient I_{rel} with length–diameter ratio b/a and effective radius of surface $ka\,(m = 1)$

(a) Alger's results   (b) $b/a = 4.0$
(c) $b/a = 1.0$ (d) Jordan's results
(e) $b/a = 0.25$
(Yang 1975)

particle velocity on a cylindrical surface around a machine varies not only with the mode number, m, the radius of the surface, r, and the wave number k, but also with the axial distance z, the length $2b$, and the diameter $2a$, of the machine. A computer program (Ellison and Yang 1971) has been written to determine the phase angles between the sound pressure and particle velocity for any given conditions. Fig. 5.2 shows that this phase angle varies considerably with the length–diameter ratio when all other conditions are the same. As expected, the phase angles at unity length–diameter ratio are found to be nearly the same as those obtained by Ellison and Moore (1969). However, it is seen that the phase angles become smaller for longer machines and greater for shorter machines. This suggests that the far field for shorter machines is further away from the machines than it is for longer machines.

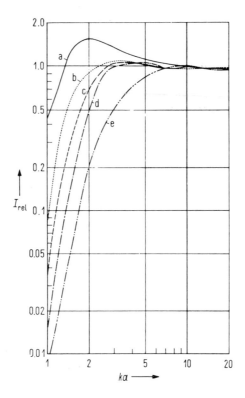

Fig. 5.4. Variation of relative sound intensity coefficient I_{rel} with length—diameter ratio b/a and effective radius of surface $ka\,(m = 2)$

(a) Alger's result   (b) $b/a = 4.0$
(c) $b/a = 1.0$ (d) Jordan's result
(e) $b/a = 0.25$
(Yang 1975)

5.4. Calculation of sound power

Based on eqn (5.12) the total sound power radiated by an electric machine can be expressed by

$$P = \int_{-\infty}^{\infty} \int_{0}^{2\pi} \tfrac{1}{2}\, \text{Re}\, \{p_i(t)\, v_i^*(t)\} r\, d\phi\, dz \qquad (5.17)$$

As we are confining our discussion to machines producing noise which is of predominantly magnetic origin, the contribution of noise power due to the vibration of the endshields is assumed negligible, i.e. the power passing through the ends is negligible, and eqn (5.17) can be simplified as follows:

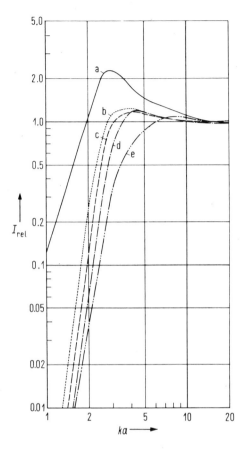

Fig. 5.5. Variation of relative sound intensity coefficient I_{rel} with length–diameter ratio b/a and effective radius of surface $ka\,(m = 3)$

(a) Alger's results   (b) $b/a = 4.0$
(c) $b/a = 1.0$ (d) Jordan's results
(e) $b/a = 0.25$
(Yang 1975)

$$P = \int_{-b}^{+b} \int_{0}^{2\pi} \tfrac{1}{2}\,\mathrm{Re}\,\{p_i(t)\,v_i^*(t)\}a\,\mathrm{d}\phi\,\mathrm{d}z$$

$$= 2\int_{0}^{b} \int_{0}^{2\pi} pv\cos\,(\theta_{p-v})a\,\mathrm{d}\phi\,\mathrm{d}z \qquad (5.18)$$

Substituting eqns (5.11), (5.15) and (5.16) into eqn (5.18), the sound power is found to be

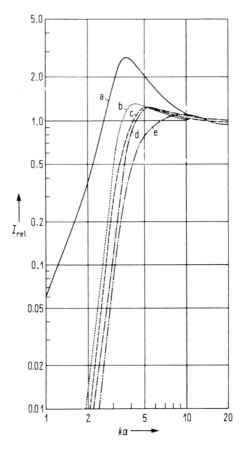

Fig. 5.6. Variation of relative sound intensity coefficient I_{rel} with length–diameter ratio b/a and effective radius of surface ka ($m = 4$)

(a) Alger's results   (b) $b/a = 4.0$
(c) $b/a = 1.0$ (d) Jordan's results
(e) $b/a = 0.25$
(Yang 1975)

$$P = \int_0^b \frac{2A_{rd}^2 \omega^3 b^2 \rho a}{\pi} (Q_{pR}^2 + Q_{pM}^2)^{1/2} (Q_{vR}^2 + Q_{vM}^2)^{1/2}$$

$$\cos \left\{ \frac{\pi}{2} + \tan^{-1} (Q_{pM}/Q_{pR}) - \tan^{-1} (Q_{vM}/Q_{vR}) \right\} dz. \quad (5.19)$$

In order to assess the efficiency of noise radiation, the average surface sound intensity radiated from the surface with travelling radial displacements of $A_{rd}e^{j(m\phi - \omega t)}$ is compared with the sound intensity produced by an inifinite plane radiator vibrating with displacements of $A_{rd}e^{j\omega t}$. The relative sound

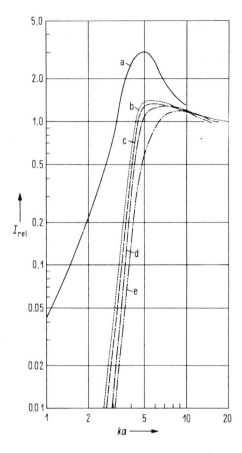

Fig. 5.7. Variation of relative sound intensity coefficient I_{rel} with length–diameter ratio b/a and effective radius of surface ka $(m = 5)$

(a) Alger's results   (b) $b/a = 4.0$
(c) $b/a = 1.0$ (d) Jordan's results
(e) $b/a = 0.25$
(Yang 1975)

intensity coefficient is defined as

$$I_{rel} = \frac{I_{av}}{I_{plane}} = \frac{(P/4\pi ab)}{2\rho c\pi^2 f^2 A_{rd}^2} \qquad (5.20)$$

where ρ is the density of the medium and c is the speed of sound in the medium. The value of ρc for air at $20°C$ is $415\,\text{Ns/m}^3$.

Substituting eqn (5.19) for P in eqn (5.20), Yang (1975) found that the I_{rel} value varies only with (a) the vibration mode, m, (b) the effective radius of surface, ka, and (c) the length–diameter ratio, b/a. The variation of relative

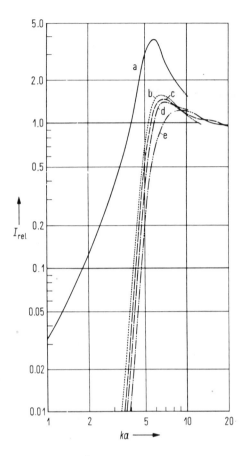

Fig. 5.8. Variation of relative sound intensity coefficient I_{rel} with length–diameter ratio b/a and effective radius of surface ka ($m = 6$)

(a) Alger's results   (b) $b/a = 4.0$
(c) $b/a = 1.0$ (d) Jordan's results
(e) $b/a = 0.25$
(Yang 1975)

sound intensity coefficient with various length–diameter ratios from 0.25 to 4.0 for mode numbers from 1 to 6 are given in Figs. 5.3 to 5.8. Based on eqn (5.20) and with the aid of Figs. 5.3 to 5.8 the sound power emission from a machine with a known surface vibration value for a vibration mode from 1 to 6 can readily be estimated (see Example 5.1).

Example 5.1

An electric machine has a standing wave surface vibration at 1500 Hz with a mode number of 2 and a maximum vibration amplitude of 1.28×10^{-7} cm.

The machine surface diameter is 16 cm and the length of the cylindrical part of the surface is 16 cm. Estimate the sound power emission due to the surface vibration at 1500 Hz.

Solution

Radius $a = 0.08$ m; half length $b = 0.08$ m, $f = 1500$ Hz. Let $c = 340$ m/s. Therefore

$$ka = \frac{\omega}{c} a = \frac{2\pi(1500)}{340}(0.08) = 2.22$$

From Fig. 5.4 for $m = 2$, $ka = 2.22$, $b/a = 1.0$, $I_{rel} = 0.85$.

The standing surface wave can be split into two travelling waves rotating in opposite directions each of which has an amplitude of vibration 0.64×10^{-7} cm. From eqn (5.20), $\rho c = 415$, $A_{rd} = 0.64 \times 10^{-9}$ m

$$P = I_{rel}(2\rho c\pi^2 f^2 A_{rd}^2)(4\pi ab)$$

$$= (0.85)(2 \times 415 \times \pi^2 \times 1500^2 \times 0.64^2 \times 10^{-18})(4\pi \times 0.08^2)$$

$$= 5.18 \times 10^{-10} \text{ W.}$$

Thus the sound power level due to this one travelling wave is

$$L_W = 10 \log \frac{P}{P_{ref}}$$

$$= 10 \log \frac{5.18 \times 10^{-10}}{10^{-12}} = 27.1 \text{ dB.}$$

The contribution of the other travelling wave with the same vibration amplitude would double the sound power. Therefore, the total sound power level at 1500 Hz is

$$L_W = 10 \log \frac{2 \times 5.18 \times 10^{-10}}{10^{-12}}$$

$$= 30.1 \text{ dB.}$$

References

ABRAMOWITZ, M. and STEGUN, I.A. (1965). *Handbook of mathematical functions*. Dover, New York.

ALGER, P.L. (1965). *The nature of induction machines*. Gordon and Breach, London.

CARTER, F.W. (1932). Magnetic noise in dynamo–electric machines. *Engineering* **134**, 548–51 and 579–81.

ELLISON, A.J. and MOORE, C.J. (1969). Calculation of acoustic power radiated by short electric machines. *Acustica* **21**, 10—15.

ELLISON, A.J. and YANG, S.J. (1971). Calculation of acoustic power radiated by an electric machine. *Acustica* **25**, 28—34.

ERDELYI, E. (1955). Predetermination of sound pressure levels of magnetic noise of polyphase induction motors. *Trans. Am. Inst. elect. Engrs* **74**, 1269—80.

JORDAN, H. (1949). Approximate calculation of the noise produced by Squirrel-cage motors. *Eng. Dig.* **10**, 222—6.

RSCHEVKIN, S.N. (1963). *The theory of sound.* Pergamon, Oxford.

YANG, S.J. (1975). Effect of length—diameter ratio on noise radiation from an electrical machine. *Acustica* **32**, 255—61.

6. Magnetic noise control

The magnetic noise emission from an electrical machine depends mainly on the radial magnetic forces in the air gap, the dynamic response of the machine structure and the radiation characteristics of the machine surface. Various methods for reducing magnetic noise are therefore related to reduction of one or more of the following:

(a) the magnetic forces;
(b) the dynamic vibration level of the machine surface;
(c) the radiation efficiency.

It should be pointed out that many measures available for noise control will often increase the cost or affect the performance of the machine. There are no simple rules applicable to all types of machines and the designer should make every effort to reduce the noise emission to a minimum within the constraints of economy and machine performance. The basic mechanisms of a number of methods for reducing the magnetic noise will be discussed in the following paragraphs.

6.1. Enlarging the air gap

For clarity, let us consider a uniform air gap of length g. The flux density wave produced by an m.m.f. wave $F(\phi, t)$ in the air gap is given by

$$B(\phi, t) \propto \frac{F(\phi, t)}{g}. \tag{6.1}$$

The radial force waves in the air gap are produced by the interaction of any two flux density waves and can be expressed as

$$\sigma_{ra}(\phi, t) \propto \frac{1}{g^2} F_1(\phi, t) F_2(\phi, t). \tag{6.2}$$

Other things being equal, the flux waves and radial force waves will be reduced by increasing the air-gap length g. As the machine vibration level A_{rd} is proportional to the force waves and the emitted sound power is proportional to A_{rd}^2, the sound power ratio for two different air-gap lengths g_1 and g_2 is given by

$$\frac{P_1}{P_2} = \frac{A_{rd, 1}^2}{A_{rd, 2}^2} = \frac{\sigma_{ra, 1}^2}{\sigma_{ra, 2}^2}. \tag{6.3}$$

TABLE 6.1. *Reduction in maximum sound power levels* achieved by various design changes (Yang 1975a)*

Noise component† (Hz) Type of machine	1039	1089	1139	1189	1239	1339
	Reduction in maximum sound power level, (dB re 10^{-12} W)					
A	10.1	1.8	9.0	0.8	7.0	7.2
B	11.2	4.9	8.9	2.5	6.7	9.5
C	9.2	6.9	11.7	7.8	14.9	13.4
D	12.2	8.7	8.3	11.9	10.3	10.1
E	10.8	1.9	5.1	4.1	8.8	13.2
F	10.4	6.5	8.6	5.1	8.4	8.5

*Sound power levels are expressed at 97.5 per cent confidence level referred to a large population and the maximum sound power levels of the standard type machines are taken as reference.
† Passband 1 per cent of centre frequency. Noise measurements were made at 2970 r/min.

Combining the above two expressions, we have

$$\frac{P_1}{P_2} = \left(\frac{g_2}{g_1}\right)^4 \qquad (6.4)$$

Thus the difference in sound power level in decibels is given by

$$L_{W,1} - L_{W,2} = 10\log_{10}\frac{P_1}{P_2} = 10\log_{10}\left(\frac{g_2}{g_1}\right)^4 \qquad (6.5)$$

Sperling (1969) showed that for a 350 kW induction motor the predominant noise at 1700 Hz was reduced by 5 dB when the air gap was increased from 1 mm to 1.5 mm, compared with a theoretical noise reduction of 7 dB obtained from eqn (6.5). It should be borne in mind that an increase in air-gap length is usually associated with a decrease in both efficiency and power factor and an increase in temperature rise for an induction machine.

6.2. Reducing pulsating noise

Homopolar flux waves are responsible for producing pulsating noise and vibration in 2-pole machines and are produced by static and dynamic rotor eccentricity and magnetic permeance variations in the stator and rotor cores. The effects of various design changes on pulsating noise were studied by Yang (1975a) for 2-pole single-phase machines and the reduction in sound emission by a number of design changes are summarized in Table 6.1. The maximum sound power levels of the 'standard' type machines (PSC 2-pole 50 Hz machines with 12 stator slots and 22 die-cast aluminium rotor bars) are taken as reference in this table. Type A machines were the same 'standard' machines except that their rotors were replaced by dynamically balanced rotors having a residual unbalance of approximately 0.5 gcm. The residual dynamic unbalance of the 'standard' rotors was approximately 1.5 to 2 gcm (rotor weight 0.68 kg). Type B machines used these balanced rotors together with stators having a special winding design to reduce the 5th and 7th harmonics as suggested by Summers (1955). The p.u. 5th and 7th harmonic contents of Type B machine stators were 0.13 and 0.09 per cent, respectively, compared with 3.4 and 2.4 per cent, respectively, for the 'standard' stator winding. Type C machines had the 'standard' stators but the standard die-cast aluminium-bar rotors were replaced by copper-bar rotors. Type D machines had the standard stators but with additional varnish dips to completely seal laminations together and to seal small core/frameband gaps. The rotors of Type D machines were made from 'scrambled' laminations to minimize the variation of magnetic permeance in the rotor core. Type E machines consisted of these 'scrambled' rotors and special stator cores which were built from cores having 50 per cent of the laminations rotated through 90°. Type F machines had balanced rotors and stators coated with epoxy resin of approximately 1 mm thickness.

Table 6.1 shows that both Type D and E machines give a considerable noise reduction for all predominant noise components. This confirms that the permeance variation in the stator and rotor cores plays an important role in noise production in 2-pole machines. Machines of Type C with copper rotor bars give a substantial reduction in noise. This may be explained by the elimination of the imperfections introduced by the die-casting process for aluminium-bar rotors. Type A machines with dynamically balanced rotors provide a considerable reduction at 1039, 1139, and 1239 Hz. Type B machines, which are similar to Type A machines but with reduced 5th and 7th harmonic contents, give slight additional noise reduction at 1089 and 1189 Hz.

The pulsating sound power at all predominant components for all seven types of machines are given in Table 6.2. The pulsating sound power is expressed as the difference between the maximum and minimum sound power for each component at 97.5 per cent confidence level.

Furthermore, 2-pole single-phase machines should be, if possible, adjusted to operate at 'balanced' condition, i.e. the phase angle between the main- and auxiliary-winding currents should be maintained at 90°. Fig. 6.1 (Yang 1975a) shows the variation of the pulsating maximum sound power level with the phase angle between the main- and auxiliary-winding currents and all the predominant pulsating noise components give the minimum sound power when the phase angle is 90°, i.e. under balanced operation. The reason for this is that the backward field would have become zero for balanced operation and all pulsating forces related to the backward field should have been eliminated. However, since there are always a series of pulsating noise components related to the forward field, noise pulsation cannot be eliminated completely even for balanced operation.

TABLE 6.2. *Pulsating sound power* from machines having various design features*
(Yang 1975a)

Noise component† (Hz) Type of machine	1039	1089	1139	1189	1239	1339
	Pulsating sound power, $P_{max} - P_{min}$, 10^{-6} W					
Standard	0.682	0.032	0.620	0.033	0.610	0.205
A	0.064	0.025	0.081	0.048	0.124	0.039
B	0.055	0.009	0.122	0.021	0.122	0.023
C	0.008	0.007	0.040	0.011	0.020	0.009
D	0.041	0.004	0.074	0.003	0.057	0.020
E	0.055	0.025	0.175	0.015	0.082	0.010
F	0.060	0.008	0.089	0.013	0.075	0.034

*Expressed at 97.5 per cent confidence level referred to a large population.
†Passband 1 per cent of centre frequency. Noise measurements were made at 2970 r/min.

In short, the following are the essential measures needed to reduce pulsating noise from 2-pole machines:

(a) the use of a dynamically balanced rotor;

(b) backward field to be kept to a minimum; and

(c) magnetic permeance variations in the stator and rotor cores to be minimized.

6.3. Skewing

Skewing either the stator or the rotor slots would make the radial forces acting on one stator lamination at a given axial position different from the forces acting on other core laminations situated at other axial positions. In other words, skewing introduces phase angles between the forces at different axial positions. Therefore, the average radial force acting on a generatrix, hence the vibration and noise level, would be reduced by skewing.

In practice, skewing is only beneficial for small a.c. machines, e.g. 100 kW or less. For large a.c. machines, especially those with ratings above 500 kW, skewing is not always useful since it causes cross-currents between rotor cage bars and could introduce torsional vibrations, leading to an increase in noise emission. For small a.c. machines, the torsional natural frequencies are often at frequencies higher than 10 kHz and the effect of tortional vibration on noise emission can usually be neglected. Jordan and Muller-Tomfelde (1961) showed that the reduction in sound level due to rotor slot skewing can be expressed as

$$L_1 - L_2 = 20 \log_{10} \left[\left\{ \sin \left(\frac{\lambda \alpha_s}{2} \right) \right\} \Big/ \left(\frac{\lambda \alpha_s}{2} \right) \right] \qquad (6.6)$$

where L_1 is the sound level without rotor skewing, L_2 is the sound level with

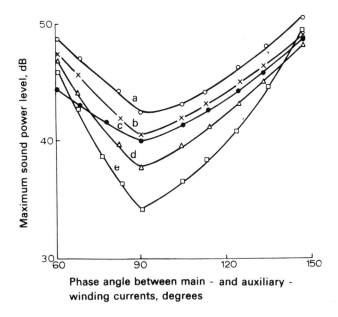

Fig. 6.1. Variation of maximum sound power level with phase angle between the main- and auxiliary-winding currents for a 2-pole single-phase motor (speed = 2970 r/min, auxiliary winding current = 0.51 A, main-winding current = 0.56 A)

(a) 1139 Hz   (b) 1189 Hz
(c) 1089 Hz   (d) 1239 Hz
(e) 1339 Hz
(Yang 1975a)

rotor skewing, λ is the number of pole pairs of the rotor m.m.f. wave contributing to the force wave concerned, and α_s is the geometrical skewing angle of the rotor slot in radians.

Sperling (1969) showed that for a 10.5 kW induction machine the predominant noise component at 700 Hz was reduced by 20 dB when using a rotor slot skewing equal to one stator slot pitch.

For d.c. machines, theoretical investigations (Mikina 1934; Astakhov 1959) show that skewing either the stator pole or the rotor slot by one or more integral rotor slot pitches is beneficial in reducing the magnetic forces and torques acting on a stator pole.

6.4. Parallel paths in stator windings

It has been shown (Ellison and Yang 1971) that rotor eccentricity introduces a series of low pole-pair radial force waves and increases the noise emission. It is therefore essential to keep the rotor eccentricity to a minimum by using strict control of manufacturing and assembling procedures. However, for economic

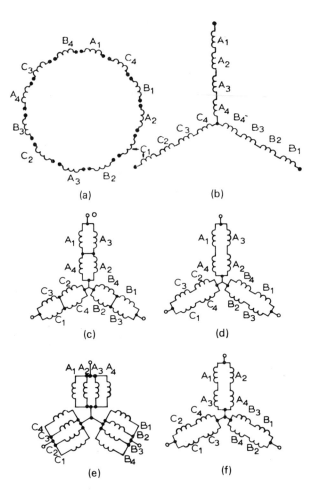

Fig. 6.2. Winding group and equalizer connections for a 4-pole machine (Ellison and Yang 1971)

(a) Distribution of pole groups
(b) All pole groups in a phase in series
(c) Two parallel paths with diametrically opposite pole groups in parallel and an equalizer
(d) As for (c) but without an equalizer
(e) Four parallel paths
(f) Two parallel paths with odd-numbered pole groups in series and without an equalizer.

reasons, and especially for mass produced machines, it is not always possible to do so. The use of parallel paths in stator windings offers another way to reduce the noise introduced by rotor eccentricity.

The basic reason for using parallel paths can be explained with the aid of Fig. 6.2, which shows the schematic diagram of 3-phase 4-pole stator winding

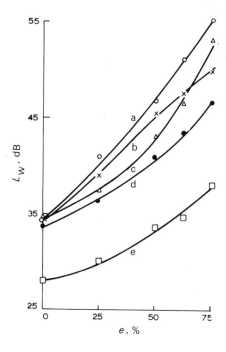

Fig. 6.3. Variation of narrow-band sound power level L_W centred at 1200 Hz with relative eccentricity e for various parallel paths and connections for a 4-pole machine (passband 6 per cent of centre frequency, constant applied voltage per winding section, total of 240 V when all in series, 97.5 per cent confidence level).

(a) All pole groups in series
(b) Two parallel paths with opposite pole groups in parallel but without equalizer
(c) Two parallel paths with odd pole groups in series and without equalizer
(d) Two parallel paths with equalizer and opposite pole groups in parallel
(e) Four parallel paths, (Ellison and Yang 1971)

arrangements having concentric-type pole windings. Let us assume that the rotor is shifted downwards. The magnetic flux per pole produced by pole winding A_1 with 1 A is less than that by winding A_3 with 1 A since the flux due to A_1 has to pass through a larger air gap. In other words, the inductance of winding A_1 is less than that of winding A_3. If the windings in each phase are connected in series, e.g. A_1, A_2, A_3, and A_4 are in series and carry the same current, then the magnetic flux produced by A_1 would be less than that produced by A_3. The unbalance of the magnetic fluxes introduces an unbalanced magnetic pull and low pole-pair force waves to cause noise and vibration. If, however, windings A_1, A_2, A_3, and A_4 are connected in parallel, as shown in Fig. 6.2(e), the current flowing in A_1 would be larger than that in A_3 since the inductance voltage drop per unit current in A_1 is smaller than that in A_3. The larger current

TABLE 6.3. *Reduction in sound power levels of a 4-pole motor achieved by different parallel paths and winding connections* (Ellison and Yang 1971)

Noise component (Hz) Type of connection	1000	1100	1200	1300	1400
	Reduction in sound power level† (dB)				
Two parallel paths, as Fig. 6.2(c) (with equalizer)	9.0	10.7	8.3	9.5	10.9
Two parallel paths, as Fig. 6.2(d) (without equalizer)	6.7	2.5	5.3	2.8	2.1
Four parallel paths, as Fig. 6.2(e)	10.5	14.8	16.9	13.1	12.6
Two parallel paths, as Fig. 6.2(f) (without equalizer)	2.5	1.5	1.8	1.1	9.3

*Constant applied voltage per winding section (total of 240 V when all in series).
†Sound power levels produced when all pole groups of each phase are in series are taken as reference. Relative eccentricity = 75 per cent.

in A_1 will offset, to a certain extent, the unbalance in magnetic flux distribution, and hence will reduce the unbalanced magnetic pull and noise emission.

Ellison and Yang (1971) studied the effects on noise radiation of different numbers of stator parallel paths and of different ways of connecting them. Using a specially constructed 4-pole machine, whose static rotor eccentricity could be adjusted precisely with negligible dynamic rotor deflection, noise measurements were made using the following stator winding connections:

(a) all pole groups in each of the phase windings in series (Fig. 6.2(b));

(b) two parallel paths with diametrically opposite pole groups in parallel and an equalizer (Fig. 6.2(c));

(c) same as (b) but without equalizer (Fig. 6.2(d));

(d) four parallel paths (Fig. 6.2(e));

(e) two parallel paths with odd numbered pole groups in series and without equalizer (Fig. 6.2(f)).

The variations with rotor eccentricity of sound power levels of the predominant components, for different parallel paths and connections are shown in Fig. 6.3. The applied voltage per winding section was kept the same and the main working flux wave was therefore kept practically constant for all these connections. If the sound power levels obtained from the connections with all pole groups in series are taken as the reference levels, the reductions in sound power levels at 75 per cent relative eccentricity produced by using different parallel paths and winding connections are shown in Table 6.3. It is seen that the connection having two parallel paths and an equalizer gives a considerable reduction in noise

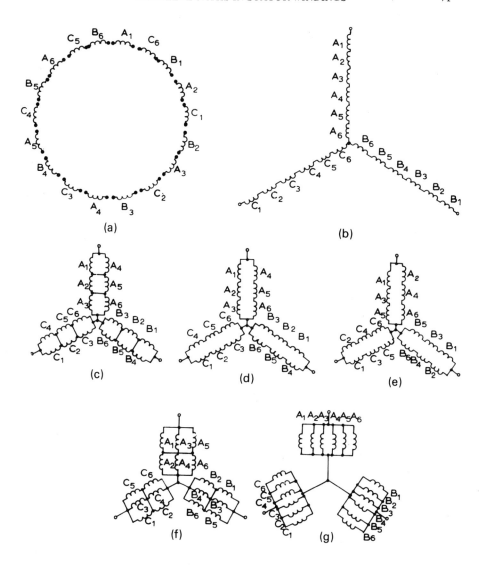

Fig. 6.4. Winding group and equalizer connections for a 6-pole machine (Ellison and Yang 1971)

(a) Distribution of pole groups
(b) All pole groups in a phase in series
(c) Two parallel paths with opposite pole groups in parallel and two equalizers
(d) The same connection as (c) but without equalizers
(e) Two parallel paths with odd-numbered pole groups in series and without equalizers
(f) Three parallel paths with two equalizers
(g) Six parallel paths

TABLE 6.4. *Reduction in sound power levels of a 6-pole motor achieved by different parallel paths and winding connection* (Ellison and Yang 1971)*

Noise component (Hz) Type of connection	700	800	900	1000	1100	1500	2400
	Reduction in sound power level[†] (dB)						
Two parallel paths as Fig. 6.4(c) (with equalizers)	4.7	3.8	3.4	5.6	13.2	7.6	4.7
Two parallel paths as Fig. 6.4(d) (without equalizers)	0.0	−1.8	−2.0	−5.0	−1.9	3.3	0.8
Two parallel paths as Fig. 6.4(e) (without equalizers)	2.7	1.3	1.6	1.6	2.8	3.1	0.7
Three parallel paths as Fig. 6.4(f) (with equalizers)	5.0	4.3	4.9	6.6	12.6	7.8	4.8
Six parallel paths as Fig. 6.4(g)	6.0	3.3	4.4	8.6	13.0	9.2	4.3

*Constant applied voltage per winding section (total of 240 V when all in series).
[†] Sound power levels produced with all pole groups of each phase in series are taken as reference. Relative eccentricity = 75 per cent.

while the same connection without an equalizer gives a much lower noise reduction. The connection with four parallel paths behaves, so far as noise is concerned, even better than the connection with two parallel paths and an equalizer.

Using a 6-pole machine, noise tests were made with the following stator winding connections:
(i) all pole groups in a phase in series (Fig. 6.4(b));
(ii) two parallel paths with opposite pole groups in parallel and two equalizers (Fig. 6.4(c));
(iii) the same connection as (ii) but without equalizers (Fig. 6.4(d));
(iv) two parallel paths with odd numbered pole groups in series and without equalizers (Fig. 6.4(e));
(v) three parallel paths with two equalizers (Fig. 6.4(f))
(iv) six parallel paths (Fig. 6.4(g)).

Table 6.4 gives the reductions in sound power levels for important noise components, at 75 per cent eccentricity produced by the different winding connections, the sound power levels produced by the connection with all pole groups of each phase in series being used as the reference. The connection having two parallel paths and two equalizers gives a considerable noise reduction while the same connection without equalizers is seen to provide no benefit in noise reduction. The connection having three parallel paths and that having six parallel paths both gave nearly the same noise reduction as that having two parallel paths and two equalizers; however, connection with two parallel paths but with the odd numbered pole groups in series and without equalizers shows very little noise reduction.

These experimental results show that the use of parallel winding paths is usually, but not always, beneficial as regards noise reduction but care must be taken to arrange the parallel circuits appropriately. The favourable connections are those having:

(a) all pole groups in each phase in parallel; and

(b) all pole groups in each phase in two parallel paths, with diametrically opposite pole groups in parallel.

Every pair of pole groups should be connected together at both ends by equalizers. Thus, in the presence of eccentricity, equalizing currents arise in the equalizers owing to the different inductances of opposite pole groups and the deleterious effects of eccentricity are reduced. As might be expected, these favourable connections for noise reduction are similar to those suggested by Krondl (1956) for reducing unbalanced magnetic pull. However, the suggestion by Novy (1961) that the most effective connection for reducing vibration is to make the number of parallel paths equal to the number of pole pairs is not always true. The use of parallel paths without equalizers seems to yield less benefit than any of the other arrangements, and, indeed, may show no advantage over the use of purely series-connected windings.

6.5. Reduction of dynamic vibrations of the machine surface

The following methods can be used to reduce the dynamic deflections of the stator surface.

(a) Mismatching the natural frequencies of the machine structures and the important exciting force frequencies. To achieve this it is necessary to determine the natural frequencies of the stator structure, the rotor system and the endshields and to compare these natural frequencies with frequencies of the main exciting force components. For variable-speed a.c. machines supplied from a solid-state variable frequency inverter, it is extermely difficult to avoid any resonance since the main exciting force frequencies vary over a wide frequency range with the variable fundamental frequency.

(b) Adjustment of the mechanical coupling between the stator core laminations and the frame so that the frame vibrations are minimized. This method is often used in large and medium-sized machines in which flexible bars (Shildneck and Wood 1953) are used to link the inner core and the outer frame. Based on a simplified two-mass spring system, the approximate ratio of the vibration amplitude of the outer frame $\hat{Y}$ to the vibration amplitude of the inner core $\hat{X}$ is given by

$$\frac{\hat{Y}}{\hat{X}} = \frac{C_k}{C_f + C_k - m_f \omega^2}$$

where C_k is the stiffness of the connection between the frame and the core, C_f is the stiffness of the frame, m_f is the mass of the frame and ω is the angular frequency of the exciting force. By adjusting the various stiffness values of the system, the outer frame vibration $\hat{Y}$ could be reduced to only a small fraction of the inner core vibration $\hat{X}$.

(c) Increasing the thickness of the stator core in order to increase its stiffness. Since the stator vibration amplitude A_{rd} is approximately inversely proportional to the cube of the thickness of the stator core and the noise emission is proportional to the square of the stator vibration amplitude, the sound power level reduction due to an increase in stator core thickness h from h_1 to h_2 is approximately given by

$$L_{W,1} - L_{W,2} = 10 \log_{10} \frac{P_1}{P_2} = 10 \log \left(\frac{h_2}{h_1}\right)^6 \text{ dB.} \qquad (6.6)$$

Corresponding to an increase in core thickness by 50%, the sound power level reduction would be approximately 10.5 dB. Although this method is effective in reducing magnetic noise, it should be borne in mind that it would increase the weight and the cost of the machine considerably. For large machines, the weight may give rise to transportation problems. Furthermore, the natural frequencies of the stator structure should be checked to ensure that no resonances occur for the thicker core design. Sometimes, radial fins are placed on the outside surface of the stator frame mainly to improve the cooling efficiency. These fins would, to a certain extent, increase the rigidity of the stator structure, and hence reduce the noise emission.

(d) Increasing the damping capacity of the machine structure by incorporating damping materials in the machine. The use of varnish or epoxy resin to completely seal stator laminations together and to seal small core/frameband gaps would increase the damping of the machine structure. Haddad and Russell (1977) found that by inserting shear damping rings in a small d.c. motor yoke, noise reductions of 10–15 dBA were obtained at both full- and no-load conditions.

(e) Increasing the exciting force mode number. Assuming the exciting force amplitude is the same for two force waves with mode numbers m_1 and m_2, the ratio of the stator deflections is given by

$$\frac{A_{rd1}}{A_{rd2}} = \frac{m_2^4}{m_1^4}. \qquad (6.7)$$

Therefore, other things being equal, the stator vibration decreases markedly when the force mode number increases. Sperling (1969) reported a considerable noise reduction for a 2-pole 630 kW squirrel-cage induction motor when the mode number of an important force wave was increased by changing the rotor slot number. The motor originally had 60 stator slots and 54 rotor slots.

Considering the force wave produced by the interaction of the fundamental stator/rotor slot permeance waves and the fundamental m.m.f. wave, the lowest force mode number can be expressed as

$$m = |Z_{st} - Z_{rt}| - 2p \tag{6.8}$$

where p is the number of pole pairs, Z_{st} is the stator slot number and Z_{rt} is the rotor slot number. For this case, $m = 60 - 54 - 2 = 4$. When the rotor slot number was changed to 44, the corresponding force mode number became $m = (60 - 44 - 2) = 14$. Since the stator deflection for $m = 14$ would be much smaller than that for $m = 4$ (see eqn (6.7)) the noise emission was greatly reduced. It should be emphasized that the above explanation is an oversimplified one. The force mode number may be affected by the stator/rotor eccentricity and dissymmetry and the sound radiation efficiency for vibrations of different mode numbers at different frequencies does not remain unchanged.

6.6. Reducing sound radiation efficiency

Yang (1975b) investigated the ratio of the average surface sound intensity radiated from a cylindrical surface with travelling radial vibration displacements of $A_{rd}e^{j(m\phi - \omega t)}$ to the sound intensity produced by an infinite plane vibrating at the same frequency ω with the same amplitude A_{rd}. The sound intensity of the plane vibrator has a definite value once the amplitude A_{rd} and the frequency ω are given. Therefore, if the plane vibrator sound intensity is taken as the reference, the ratio can be taken as the relative sound radiation efficiency.

Yang (1975b) has shown that the relative sound radiation efficiency varies with

(a) the vibration mode number, m;
(b) the effective radius of surface, ka; and
(c) the length–diameter ratio of the machine, b/a, where k is equal to ω/c and c is the speed of sound, a is the machine radius and b is half of the machine length.

Figs. 5.3 to 5.8 in Chapter 5 gave some results for the variation of the relative sound radiation efficiency with these factors for mode numbers of 1 to 6 and length–diameter ratios of 0.25 to 4.0. In these figures the results obtained by Jordan (1949) based on a spherical source and the results obtained by Alger (1965) based on an infinite long cylindrical surface were also given for comparison. As expected, Jordan's results were seen to be smaller than Yang's results for unity–diameter ratio while Alger's results were found to give higher values compared with Yang's results for a length–diameter ratio of 4. These figures also show that, for most cases, the radiation efficiency for shorter machines is lower than that for longer ones. Furthermore, for low *ka* values, the radiation efficiency for lower mode numbers is higher than that for higher mode numbers.

Therefore, in choosing the length and diameter of an electrical machine for minimum noise emission, the combination of a shorter length together with a larger diameter is preferred to one with longer length and smaller diameter. Furthermore, it is advisable to choose the stator/rotor slot numbers to ensure that the important force components have higher mode numbers.

It should be pointed out that the choice of the stator/rotor slot numbers is not at all free. Consideration should be given to stray losses, cogging torques, synchronous and asynchronous torques, the cost, and the machine performance. Furthermore, care should be taken that the change in slot numbers would not bring resonances to the machine structure due to the corresponding change in the exciting force frequencies.

Although many rules have been suggested for the choice of stator/rotor slot numbers, none seems to work well for all types of machines. Jordan (1952) pointed out that for minimum noise emission, there were no absolutely 'good' slot combinations and the choice should be made in the knowledge of the magnetic force wave components, the mechanical behaviour of the machine structure and the radiation properties of the machine surface. Hore (1970) considered 'sticking to the rules' for stator/rotor slot combinations a first-class way of finding trouble and suggested that what was important was not the exciting frequencies as such, but keeping these frequencies away from the mechanical natural frequencies of the machine structure.

References

ALGER, P.L. (1965). *The nature of induction machines.* Gordon & Breach, New York.

ASTAKHOV, N.V. (1959). Magnetic noise in universal commutator micromotors. *Elektrichestvo* **1**, 41–5.

ELLISON, A.J. and YANG, S.J. (1971). Effects of rotor eccentricity on acoustic noise from induction machines. *Proc. Instn elect. Engrs* **118**, 174–84.

HADDAD, S.D. and RUSSELL, M.F. (1977). Noise sources of small electrical machines and some control methods. *Proc. 9th Int. Cong. Acoustics,* Madrid, paper E-57, p. 207.

HORE, R.A. (1970). Contribution to the discussion of 'Acoustic noise and vibration of rotating electric machines' by Ellison, A.J. and Moore, C.J. *Proc. Instn elect. Engrs* **117**, 128.

JORDAN, H. (1949). Approximate calculation of the noise produced by squirrel-cage motors. *Eng. Dig.* **10**, 222–6.

——— (1952). Uber das magnetische gerausch von Drehstrom-Asynchron-maschinen. *Elektrotech. Z. ETZ A* **73**, 620–5.

JORDAN, H. and MÜLLER-TOMFELDE, H. (1961). Akustische Wirkung der Schrängung bei Drehstrom-Asynchronmaschinen mit Käfigläufern. *Elektrotech. Z. ETZ A* **82**, 788–92.

KRONDL, M. (1956). Les vibrations radiales antoexcitees du rotor de machines a induction a voies d'enroulement paralleles. *Bull. Ass. Suisse Electn.* **47**, 581–8.

MIKINA, S.J. (1934). The effect of skewing and pole spacing on magnetic noise in electric machinery. *Trans. Am. Soc. mech. Engrs* **55**, 711–20.

NOVY, F. (1961). Chveni statoru asynchronnich stroju. *Elektrotech. Obz.* **50**, 364–7.

SHILDNECK, L.P. and WOOD, A.J. (1953). Reduction of noise produced by small and medium 2-pole turbine generators. *Trans. Am. Inst. elect. Eng.* **72**, 36–40.

SPERLING, VON P.G. (1969). Erfahrungen bei der Vorausberechnung elektro-magnetisch erzeugter Maschinengerausche. *Siemens Z.* **43**, 894–8.

SUMMERS, E.W. (1955). Vibration in 2-pole induction motors related to slip frequency. *Trans. Am. Inst. elect. Eng.* **74**, Part III, 69–72.

YANG, S.J. (1975*a*). Acoustic noise from small 2-pole single-phase induction machines. *Proc. Instn elect. Engrs* **122**, 1391–6.

—————— (1975*b*). Effect of length–diameter ratio on noise radiation from an electrical machine. *Acustica* **32**, 255–61.

7. Suppressing noise of mechanical origins

7.1. Motor bearing noise characteristics

Sleeve bearings are usually not an important noise contributor for an electrical machine. However, the noise from, or excited by, rolling bearings may be important, especially for small high-speed machines with a rating of less than 20 kW. Table 7.1 (Ellison and Yang 1970) shows the mean sound level referred to a 3 m radius in A weighting for 20 nominally identical electrical machines with a rating of 0.24 kW. Ten of these machines were equipped with sleeve bearings while the other ten had ball bearings. It is clear that the ball bearing motors were much noisier than the sleeve bearing motors and the ball bearings in the machines played an important role in noise generation. It has been found (Tallian and Gustafsson 1965) that the ball bearing quality grade affects motor noise emission in the frequency range from 50 Hz to 5000 Hz considerably.

The noise from rolling bearings is related to the following factors:

(a) the accuracy of the bearing elements: track geometry, the sphericity of the rolling elements, size variation from element to element, surface roughness both on the tracks and on the rolling elements;

(b) the presence of dirt and foreign matters;

(c) the lubrication conditions;

(d) the amount of residual internal clearance in the bearing after mounting;

(e) the natural frequencies of the outer ring and the running speed;

(f) the form and alignment of the housing;

(g) the load and the operating temperature.

Rolling bearing noise consists of both broad-band noise and discrete components. For ball bearings, the frequencies of the most probable components of bearing noise and their causes are as follows.

TABLE 7.1. *Variation of mean sound level (A) referred to 3 m radius between nominally identical machines (upper limit at 97.5 per cent confidence level) (Ellison and Yang 1970)*

Motor No. Bearings	Mean sound level (A) (dBA)									
	1	2	3	4	5	6	7	8	9	10
Sleeve	26.1	29.9	27.9	24.2	31.3	28.7	24.6	27.8	28.7	29.9
Ball	31.8	37.5	34.2	35.1	32.4	37.1	40.4	31.5	35.9	36.8

(a) Owing to the unbalance or eccentricity of the inner ring, there is a noise component at the rotor rotational frequency:

$$f_{rt} = n_{rt} \tag{7.1}$$

where n_{rt} is the rotor speed in r/s.

(b) An irregularity in the cage, i.e. the ball separator, causes noise at the cage speed frequency (Harris 1957)

$$f_{ca} = n_{ca} \simeq n_{rt} \left(\frac{r_{i,r}}{r_{i,r} + r_{o,r}} \right) \tag{7.2}$$

where $r_{i,r}$ is the radius of contact surface between inner ring and balls and $r_{o,r}$ is the radius of contact surface between outer ring and balls. In most cases, cage speed n_{ca} is equal to $0.4 n_{rt}$.

(c) A defect on the outer ring causes noise at the frequency of ball passage over the outer ring.

$$f_{o,r} = Z_{ba} f_{ca} \approx Z_{ba} n_{rt} \left(\frac{r_{i,r}}{r_{i,r} + r_{o,r}} \right) \tag{7.3}$$

where Z_{ba} is the number of balls.

(d) The stiffness of the bearing under load varies with the relative position of the ball elements with respect to the line of load. The elastic deflection of the contacts in the bearing, when one ball is directly in the line of load, see Fig. 7.1(a), differs from that when two balls are equally spaced from the line of load, see Fig. 7.1(b). The variation in the stiffness causes noise at the frequency of ball passage over the outer ring and its harmonics.

$$f_{ba} = i Z_{ba} f_{ca} \approx i Z_{ba} n_{rt} \left(\frac{r_{i,r}}{r_{i,r} + r_{o,r}} \right) \tag{7.4}$$

where i is any positive integer. The magnitude of these components depends on the load and the internal clearance of the bearing (Tallian and Gustafsson 1965).

(e) The surface roughness excites noise at the natural frequencies of the radial and axial vibration of the outer ring (Tallian and Gustafsson 1965; Lohmann 1953). It should be noted that the fit between the bearing and the housing can affect the values of these natural frequencies. Cylindrical roller bearings usually emit more noise than ball bearings, as sliding is likely to occur between the rollers and the tracks.

Sleeve bearings in general produce less noise than ball bearings. They excite some high frequency noise due to the surface roughness and the changes in lubrication conditions. Their possible discrete noise components are as follows.

(a) Rotor unbalance or eccentricity causes noise at the rotor rotational

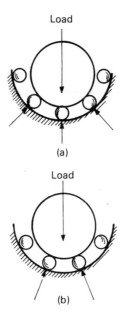

Fig. 7.1. (a) Elastic deflection of the contacts when one ball is directly in the line of load. (b) Elastic deflection of the contacts when two balls are equidistant from the line of load.

frequency:

$$f_{rt} = n_{rt}.$$ (7.5)

(b) The excitation from the axial grooves causes noise at the groove passage frequency (Campbell 1963)

$$f_{gr} = n_{rt} G$$ (7.6)

where G is the number of axial grooves.

(c) Bearing oil whirl causes noise and vibration with a frequency equal to a critical speed of the rotor. It is caused by a self-excited vibration due to oil film instability and occurs when the machine speed is more than twice the first rotor critical speed (Smith 1963). Sometimes, noise of half-speed whirl exists at half the rotor rotational frequency.

7.2. Motor bearing noise reduction

Apart from the proper choice of the bearing type and size, the following design measures would be beneficial in reducing rolling bearing noise.

(a) To apply an axial preload on the bearing by means of coil springs: the axial preload can reduce vibrations due to uncontrolled motions of loose

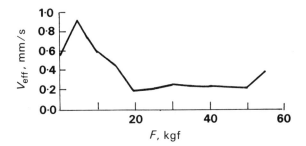

Fig. 7.2. Variation of vibration velocity V_{eff} in the axial direction with the axial preload F on the bearings measured on a 4-pole motor of shaft height 132 mm with a no-load speed of 1500 r/min (Solhardt 1968)

$$V_{eff} = \lim_{T \to \infty} \sqrt{\left\{ \frac{1}{T} \int_0^T V^2(t)\,dt \right\}}$$

rolling elements and modify the elastic properties of the bearing. The optimal level of axial preload should be determined by test. Fig. 7.2 shows an example of the variation of axial vibration with axial preload for a 4-pole machine.

(b) To add elastic damping elements in the housing support structure: the introduction of damping in bearing support structures is usually beneficial in reducing noise and vibration at frequencies above several hundred hertz.

(c) To use bearings having cages made from synthetic plastic-type materials or solid-machined cages: these bearings run more quietly at high speeds.

(d) To use bearings having shields or seals to prevent ingress of dirt and foreign matter under normal operating conditions.

(e) To mismatch the natural frequencies of the bearing outer ring and the bearing support structure with the important mechanical and electrical exciting force frequencies.

(f) To keep the bearing angular misalignment to a minimum. Fig. 7.3 shows an example of the effect of bearing angular misalignment on mechanical noise (Pittroff 1971). For deep groove ball bearings, an angular misalignment greater than 10′ is not permissible. For angular contact ball bearings, the angular misalignment should not exceed 2′ since it stresses angular contact ball bearings to a higher degree than deep groove ball bearings (Rienecker 1976).

(g) To choose a suitable clearance group. In choosing the clearance grade, it is necessary to take into account the effect of machine temperature rise on clearance. Kutcher and Pavlov (1973) showed that the actual working clearance should be kept close to zero for minimum bearing induced vibration. For a motor equipped with bearings having an outer diameter of 72 mm and an internal clearance of $10 \sim 24\,\mu m$ between the rolling elements and the rings, the machine vibration was found to be minimum when the fit between

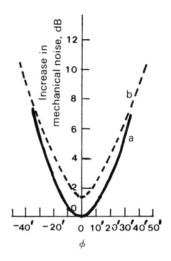

Fig. 7.3. Angular misalignment ϕ due to imperfections of bearing housing positions, and an example of its effect on mechanical noise (Pittroff 1971)

(a) C2 clearance   (b) Normal clearance

the bearing outer ring and the housing was an interference of $10 \sim 15\,\mu m$ (Pavlov 1973). The clearance groups preferred for bearings in electric motors are the normal clearance group and the clearance group larger than normal C3 (Rienecker 1976).

(h) For electrical machines used in certain domestic appliances and machine tools which have to meet special low noise and vibration specifications, precision bearings with a fine finish hone on the tracks can be used. For these bearings, it would be necessary to choose a suitable grease to avoid grease noise. Harris (1976) found that the noise induced by the greases used in electric motor grade ball bearings for dishwashers was of the psychologically irritating 'snap, crackle, pop, and slurp' type of noise.

For motors used for domestic gas heating appliances, Hutton *et al.* have developed a low noise hydrodynamic grease bearing (Hutton, Binns, Middleton and Woolley 1976). For small motors with output ratings below 1 kW, SKF (Electrical Review 1972) has developed a method of mounting the bearings and the bearing housings inside the stator winding. It was claimed that the accuracy of this mounting gave greater precision of rotor positioning and a noise reduction of 4 dBA, compared with that produced by an equivalent sized conventional motor with the cooling fan removed.

7.3. Brush-commutator noise characteristics

Brush noise is caused by the sliding contact of current brushes against commutator segments or slip rings in certain types of electrical machines, e.g. d.c.

machines, slip-ring induction machines, synchronous machines and a.c. commutator machines. The brush–slip-ring system serves the function of current transfer and current switching. The noise generated by brush–slip-ring systems is usually of secondary importance. However, the sliding process in brush–commutator systems for small a.c. commutator machines and large d.c. machines can be an important noise source.

The noise from a brush–commutator system is related to the following factors:

(a) the materials used for the commutator segments and the brushes;

(b) the pressure at the brush–commutator interface;

(c) the current load carried by the system;

(d) the brush and commutator surface conditions and the coefficient of friction between the brush and the commutator;

(e) the coefficient of friction between the brush and the brush holder;

(f) the details of the brushgear design, e.g. the clearance between the brush and the brush holder and the rigidity of the brush holder;

(g) the sparking of the brush–commutator system;

(h) the operating environment, e.g. humidity.

Most of these factors are interrelated. For example, the coefficient of friction of the brush-commutator sliding contact for a given system is a complex function of the current load and may vary by as much as 5 to 1 (Wakeley 1974). Therefore, analytical and experimental studies on brush noise are either difficult or expensive. In the literature very little information is available on brush noise.

Owing to the surface roughness and irregularity on both commutator and brush surfaces, broad-band noise is produced by the sliding process. Intermittent sparkings can add unsteady noise over a wide frequency range. The discrete noise components caused by brush vibrations are at the following frequencies:

$$f_b = iZ_c n_{rt} \qquad (7.7)$$

where i is any positive integer, Z_c is the number of commutator segments and n_{rt} is the machine speed in r/s.

7.4. Brush-commutator noise reduction

For a given operating environment, suitable design efforts can reduce brush noise. Astakhov (1959) studied the variation of brush noise with a number of brushgear parameters for single-phase commutator machines having ratings of 25 W to 50 W running at speeds of 3500 to 5000 r/min with conventional commutator and brush materials. Fig. 7.4(b) shows the variation of brush noise with the angle α between the brush axis and the radial line passing through the contact point. It suggests that the angle α should be kept to zero for minimum noise emission. Fig. 7.4(c) shows that brush noise is a function of the brush end length, l_1, from the bottom of the brush holder to the centre of the contact

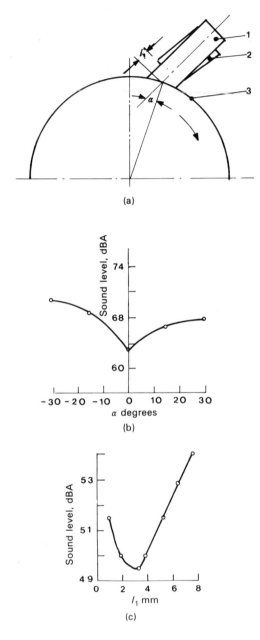

Fig. 7.4 (a) Geometry of brush–commutator system. (1) Brush (2) Brush holder (3) Commutator surface. α Angle of brush inclination, l_1 External brush length outside brush holder. (b) Variation of sound level with angle of brush inclination. (c) Variation of sound level with external brush length (Astakhov 1959)

surface. l_1 and α are defined in Fig. 7.4(a). The optimal length l_1 for minimum noise emission is in the range of 2 to 4 mm. Astakhov found that brush noise varied with brush pressure and the optimum pressure was 400 to 450 g/cm². He also showed that brush noise varied with the clearance between the brush and the brush holder and a clearance of 0.2 mm gave the minimum noise emission. These figures present some guidance for designing small machine brushgears.

To minimize the brush commutator noise from large machines or from small high speed machines, the above figures are no longer valid. It is necessary for the manufacturer to carry out a series of tests to obtain the information about the suitable brush material and other brushgear parameters to meet the noise specifications.

The most common brush material is copper graphite, which can handle a relatively high current density of 220 kA/m² with low voltage drop, e.g. 0.25 V per brush. However, the contact operating speed is limited to 30 m/s for a reasonable brush life. For high speeds up to 75 m/s, electrographite or natural graphite brushes can be used. Carbon-fibre brushes have recently been developed for high speed small commutator motors (Bates and Carter 1976).

One method for controlling brush-commutator noise for medium-sized and large machines is to use covers to enclose the brush commutator end of the machine. Wakeley (1974) studied the method for a 500 kW (670 hp) 980 r/min d.c. motor having 6 brush arms, 5 brushes per arm and 306 commutator segments. The mean difference between the octave-band sound pressure levels centred at 2000 Hz and measured at 17 positions around the machine with and without the brush commutator covers was 6 dB.

7.5. Rotor unbalance noise characteristics

Rotor unbalance gives rise to dynamic rotor vibration and eccentricity which in turn cause noise emission from the stator, the rotor, and the rotor support structures. The mechanical exciting frequency due to rotor centrifugal force is equal to the rotor rotational frequency and can cause noise and vibration at frequencies equal to an integer times the rotor rotational frequency if these frequencies coincide with the natural frequencies of the rotor support structures. Thus, the frequency of the rotor unbalance noise can be expressed as

$$f_{un} = in_{rt} \qquad (7.8)$$

where i is any positive integer and n_{rt} is the machine speed in r/s. For most small and medium-sized electrical machines, the direct airborne noise at the rotational frequency is low. However, rotor unbalance may cause considerable structure-borne noise.

The dynamic rotor eccentricity in an electrical machine due to rotor unbalance introduces additional magnetic forces. Voller (1965) found that for a 4-pole 3 kW motor the vibration velocity at 25 Hz, measured on a test rig, increased

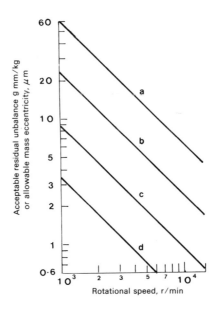

Fig. 7.5. Acceptable residual unbalance (VDI 2060, 1966)

(a) For small electrical armatures.
(b) For rigid turbogenerators, medium and large electrical armatures with special requirements and for small electrical armatures.
(c) For small electrical armatures with special requirements.
(d) For armatures of precision grinders.

from 50 μm/s to 400 μm/s and then to 900 μm/s when the additional rotor
unbalance increased from zero to 15 gcm and then to 30 gcm, respectively. In
2-pole machines, dynamic rotor eccentricity causes homopolar fluxes (Yang
1975) which introduce pulsating magnetic forces and pulsating noise emission.

7.6. Rotor unbalance noise reduction

In order to reduce the noise caused by rotor unbalance, it is essential to keep the
dynamic rotor unbalance within an appropriate limit. There are several rotor
balance criteria in common use which are based on the practical experience of
many machinery manufacturers. Fig. 7.5 (Muster 1968) gives the acceptable
residual unbalance per unit of rotor mass in gmm/kg or the allowable mass
eccentricity in micrometers for various operating speeds with various balancing
grades, based on the code of practice VDI 2060 (Muster 1968; VDI 2060 1966).

   VDI 2060 is intended only for a 'rigid' rotor, i.e. for a rotor whose operating
speed n_{rt} is much less than the first critical speed n_{cr}. For a practical flexible
rotor operating below its first critical speed, Woodcock (1975) suggested that

$$e_f \not> e\{1 - (n_{rt}/n_{cr})^2\} \tag{7.9}$$

where e_f is the allowable mass eccentricity for the practical flexible rotor and e is the allowable mass eccentricity for a 'rigid' rotor.

A machine well balanced on works test may exhibit unacceptable noise and vibration at site when it is coupled to other equipment (Pomfret 1973). The reasons are (a) changes in bearing support stiffness and vibration mode shapes, (b) coupling misalignment or unbalanced couplings, and (c) unbalance of the coupled equipment.

It is therefore beneficial to carry out balancing jobs *in situ*, i.e. to balance the complete rotating system under actual operating conditions.

It should be pointed out that rotor balancing cannot cure the mechanical noise at twice the rotor rotational frequency for a machine rotor having a non-uniform stiffness, e.g. a 2-pole generator rotor whose bending stiffnesses about the two rotor principal axes differ due to slotting. In this case, the rotor deflection changes periodically at twice the rotor rotational frequency and the noise and vibration at this frequency may become unacceptably high if the bearing support structure or the machine structure has a natural frequency equal to, or near, twice rotor rotational frequency. Additional longitudinal dummy slots can be cut in the rotor to equalize the rotor bending stiffness and should be filled with steel bars to give a satisfactory magnetic flux path. To cut narrow slots transversely across the two pole faces is also beneficial in equalizing the rotor stiffness (Consterdine 1968).

References

ASTAKHOV, N.V. (1959). Brush noise in miniature single-phase commutator motors. *Electrichestvo* **9**, 46–50.

BATES, J.J. and CARTER, J. (1976). The use of carbon-fibre brush in small commutator motors. IEE Conf. Publ. 36, 11–14.

CAMPBELL, J. (1963). Electric-motor noise. *Machine design,* **35**, pp. 139–58.

CONSTERDINE, E.W. (1968). Mechanical design problems of turbo-generators. *Turbine-generator engineering,* AEI, pp. 126–34.

Electrical Review (1972). Motor bearing arrangements reduce noise and vibration. *Elect. Rev.* **190**, 577–8.

ELLISON, A.J. and YANG, S.J. (1970). Acoustic noise measurements on nominally identical small electrical machines. *Proc. Instn elect. Engrs* **117**, 555–60.

HARRIS, C.M. (1957). *Handbook of noise control.* McGraw-Hill, New York.

HARRIS, J.F. (1976). The measurement of grease noise in electric motor grade ball bearings. *IEE Trans. Ind. Appl.,* IA-12, 359–63.

HUTTON, S.J., BINNS, K.J., MIDDLETON, A.H., and WOLLEY, R.W. (1976). The development of an integrated design of motor-driven fan with very low noise level. *IEE Conf. Publ.* 35, 43–6.

KUTCHEV, R.I. and PAVLOV, A.G. (1973). Influence of rolling-bearing clearance on vibration. *Russ. Eng. J.* **53**, 32–5.

LOHMANN, G. (1953). Noise investigation of rolling bearings. *Eng. Dig.* **14**, 204–9.

MUSTER, D. (1968). International standardization in mechanical vibration and shock. *J. environ. Sci.* 8–12.

PITTROFF, H. (1971). Reliable and noiseless bearings for small electric motors. *Technica* **20**, 2499–504.

POMFRET, B. (1973). Vibration of rotating electrical machines due to residual mechanical unbalance, *LSE Eng. Bull.* **12**, 1–6.

RIENECKER, L. (1976). Some factors governing the bearing selection for standard and series electric motors. *Ball roll. Bear. Eng.* **2**, 52–6.

SMITH, D.M. (1963), Dynamic characteristics or turbine journal bearings. Proceedings of the Lubrication and Wear Convention (I. Mech. E.), Bournemouth, paper 8.

SOLHARDT, K. (1968). Low-vibration electrical machines of the IEC series. *Brown Boveri Rev.* **55**, 664–71.

TALLIAN, T.E. and GUSTAFSSON, O.G. (1965). Progress in rolling bearing vibration research and control. *Trans. Am. Soc. Lubricat. Engrs* **8**, 195–207.

VDI 2060 (1966). Translation of *Criteria for assessing the state of balance of rotating rigid bodies.* Peter Penegrinus, Stevenage.

VÖLLER, R. (1965). Vibration testing of electric motors for machine tools. *Eng. Dig.* **26**, 95–7 and 107.

WAKELEY, K. (1974). Noise problems on large rotating machines. *Proc. Int. Conf. Electrical Machines,* London, B4–1 to B4–17.

WOODCOCK, J.S. (1975). Balancing criteria for high speed rotors with flexible couplings. *Proc. Conf. Vibrations and Noise in Pumps, Fan and Compressor Installations,* Southampton, pp. 107–114.

YANG, S.J. (1975). Acoustic noise from 2-pole single-phase induction machines. *Proc. Instn elect. Engrs* **122**, 1391–6.

8. Controlling noise of aerodynamic origin

Cooling air or gas flow in electrical machines may give rise to significant aerodynamic noise emission. Aerodynamic noise consists, in general, of discrete noise components and broad-band unpitched noise. The former is caused by periodical pressure disturbances due to rotating components such as fan blades and stationary obstacles in the fluid stream. The latter is associated with the random pressure disturbances in a fast moving fluid stream. In the following paragraphs we shall discuss, with special reference to electric motors, various practical measures for suppression of aerodynamic noise.

8.1. Controlling the noise due to mounting ribs

For motors equipped with cooling fans, there are usually mounting ribs and other obstacles in the air stream near the fan blades. King (1944) found that the vortex noise, at frequency f_v, produced by the radial mounting arms installed before a fan in the air stream of a circular duct, modulated with the fan blade frequency noise at frequency f_t, resulted in discrete noise components at frequencies of $f_v \pm f_t$. The vortex frequency can be approximately expressed by

$$f_v = 0.185 \frac{v}{D} \text{ Hz} \tag{8.1}$$

where v is the air stream velocity (m/s) and D is the diameter of the mounting arm (m). The fan blade frequency f_t is given by

$$f_t = \frac{Z_t n_t}{60} \text{ Hz} \tag{8.2}$$

where Z_t is the number of fan blades and n_t is the fan speed (r/min). King found that when the arms were changed from a circular to an aerofoil cross-section, i.e. bull nose and tapering tail, the vortex frequency f_v was no longer detectable.

Ploner and Herz (1969) tested the effect of axial rib design on fan blade frequency noise and found that a rib design of triangular cross section gave an approximate 8 dB noise reduction at the blade frequency compared with the rectangular cross-section rib. They also showed that an increase in the distance between the fan blade tip and the rib from 6 mm to 10 mm resulted in a noise reduction of more than 4 dB for most ribs tested. Rentzsch (1961) recommended that the minimum distance δ (mm) between the fan blades and a fixed obstacle should be as follows:

$$\delta = u^2/30 \qquad (8.3)$$

where u is the fan blade tip speed (m/s).

8.2. Suppressing the air duct siren noise and the use of an enclosure

In medium-sized and large electrical machines, cooling air passing through the rotor/stator ventilation duct channels produces a siren noise component at the following frequency:

$$f_{si} = \frac{Z_{rt}n_{rt}}{60} \text{ Hz} \qquad (8.4)$$

where Z_{rt} is the rotor slot number and n_{rt} is the rotor speed (r/s). An analytical method for the calculation of this siren noise has been presented by Talaat (1957). One effective way to reduce it is to place acoustical absorbing material close to the opening of the stator radial ventilation ducts. For an induction motor, Ploner (1976) used sillan rock-wool and obtained a noise reduction of 10 dB at the frequency given by eqn (8.4). Another measure for reducing the siren noise involves the use of half round rotor bars.

The use of an enclosure and/or a closed circuit ventilation system can offer a significant noise reduction up to 20 dB or more. In estimating the noise reduction achieved by a complete enclosure, it is necessary to take into account the fact that, owing to the reflection of enclosure walls, the sound pressure level inside an enclosure is higher than that at the same points but without the enclosure. This build-up in sound pressure level can be calculated approximately by the following expression (Zeller 1950):

$$\Delta L_{\text{B.U.}} = 10 \log_{10}\left(\frac{1}{\alpha}\right) \text{ dB} \qquad (8.5)$$

where α is the sound absorption coefficient of the inner surface of the enclosure for a particular frequency. The transmission loss of an enclosure for the frequency range of 100 Hz to 3000 Hz can be estimated by (Cremer 1950)

$$\Delta L_{\text{T.L.}} = 14(1 + \log_{10}M) \text{ dB} \qquad (8.6)$$

where M is the mass of the enclosure wall per unit area (kg/m^2).

The overall noise reduction of an enclosure is thus equal to

$$\Delta L = \Delta L_{\text{T.L.}} - \Delta L_{\text{B.U.}}$$

It should be emphasized that the transmission loss through an enclosure varies with frequency. For effective low-frequency noise reduction, enclosure wall stiffness should be high, while, for high frequency noise reduction, an increase in both wall stiffness and damping is necessary. For some practical cases an increase in the mass per unit area is beneficial.

However, based on eqn (8.6), each doubling of enclosure wall thickness will give an increase of only 4.2 dB in transmission loss. A more efficient and economical way is to reduce the build-up effect by lining the inner surface of the enclosure with sound absorbent materials, such as rock wool and glass fibres. As an example, let us estimate the noise reduction at 1000 Hz for an enclosure having 1 mm thick sheet-steel walls. The coefficient of absorption of the steel sheet at 1000 Hz is 0.03 and the sheet mass is 7.86 kg/m^2. If the inner surface of the enclosure is lined with 30 mm thick rock wool with a coefficient of absorption of 0.55 at 1000 Hz and a mass of 3 kg/m^2, estimate the increase in noise reduction with the rock wool lining.

For the 1 mm thick steel sheet enclosures the sound pressure level build up at 1000 Hz is

$$\Delta L_{\text{B.U.}} = 10 \log_{10} \left(\frac{1}{0.03} \right) = 15.23 \text{ dB.}$$

The transmission loss is

$$\Delta L_{\text{T.L.}} = 14(1 + \log_{10} 7.86)$$
$$= 26.54 \text{ dB.}$$

The overall noise reduction at 1000 Hz is

$$\Delta L = 26.54 - 15.23 = 11.31 \text{ dB.}$$

If the inner surface is lined with 30 mm thick rock wool

$$\Delta L_{\text{B.U.}} = 10 \log_{10} \left(\frac{1}{0.55} \right) = 2.60 \text{ dB,}$$

$$\Delta L_{\text{T.L.}} = 14\{1 + \log_{10}(7.86 + 3.0)\}$$
$$= 28.50 \text{ dB.}$$

The overall noise reduction becomes

$$\Delta L = 28.50 - 2.60 = 25.90 \text{ dB.}$$

Thus the increase in noise reduction at 1000 Hz with the lining is $(25.90 - 11.31) = 14.59$ dB.

8.3. Air inlet and outlet noise control

The use of air inlet and outlet silencers with acoustically absorbing materials is in many cases the most effective way to reduce aerodynamic noise. The noise

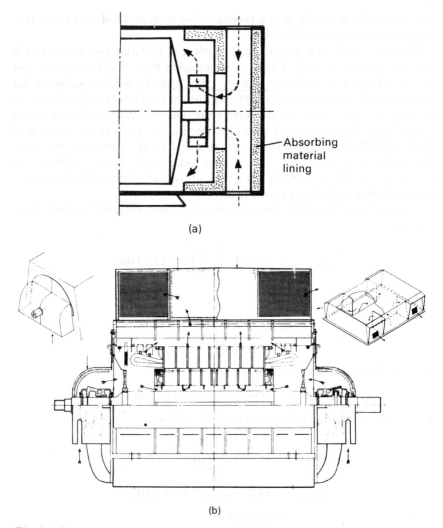

Fig. 8.1. Examples of inlet and outlet silencer arrangements

(a) An air inlet silencer.
(b) A 5 MW 4-pole 11 kV induction motor with air inlet and outlet silencers (Bone and Schwarz 1973).

attenuation, expressed as the difference in sound pressure level between the entrance and the exit of a duct lined with sound absorbent walls, can be estimated by (Schulz 1964)

$$\Delta L = (1.3 \sim 1.5)\alpha l \frac{U}{A} \text{ dB} \qquad (8.7)$$

where α is the sound absorption coefficient of the lining material, l the length of the duct (m), U the noise absorbent perimeter of the duct (m) and A the cross-sectional area of the duct (m^2). Fig. 8.1 shows some air inlet and outlet silencing arrangements.

8.4. Cooling fan noise control

The sound power level in C weighting emitted by a fan used in electrical machines can be estimated by (Francoise 1970)

$$L_P = 70 \log_{10} D + 50 \log_{10} \left(\frac{N}{1000}\right) + K \text{ dB} \qquad (8.8)$$

where D is the diameter of the fan blade (m), N is the speed (r/min) and K is a constant depending upon the type of the fan. For fans with welded steel sheet blades used in electrical machines, $K = 107$. For fans with profiled blades and operating near their optimal efficiency point, $K = 94$. It should be emphasized that the sound power emission of a fan depends not only on the fan design but also on its operating conditions.

Apart from the proper choice of fan type and blade profile design, the following measures are, to a certain extent, helpful in reducing fan noise.

8.4.1. Use of unevenly spaced fan blades

The use of unevenly spaced fan blades reduces the strength of the regular pressure disturbances caused by evenly spaced fan blades at the blade frequency. However, tests have shown that the overall noise level such as sound level in A or C weighting generated by a fan having unevenly spaced blades is practically the same as that generated by a fan having evenly spaced blades. Nevertheless, subjective annoyance is reduced by this method since the level of the most predominant blade frequency noise component is reduced by unequal blade spacing (see Fig. 8.2).

Mellin and Sovran (1970) recommended use of the following expression for fixing the blade spacings:

$$(S_n') = \frac{360}{B + j\beta \cos\left[\frac{2\pi j}{B}(n - \frac{1}{2})\right]} \qquad (8.9)$$

where S is the angle in degrees between adjacent blades, B is the number of blades, n is an integer from 1 to B, j is an integer which is greater than or equal to 1, and β is a parameter representing the degree of non-uniformity in the blade spacing and is greater than or equal to zero. Since the sum of these blade space

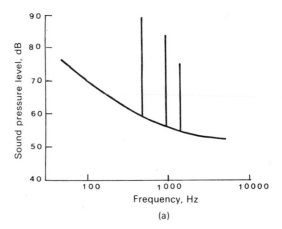

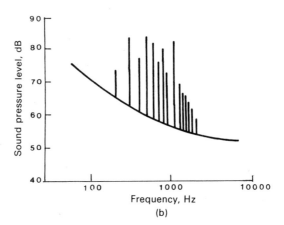

Fig. 8.2. Effects of unequal blade spacing on fan noise spectra (Mellin and Sovran 1970)

(a) Equal blade spacing.
(b) Unequal blade spacing.

angles does not yield exactly 360°, the spacing should be finally adjusted according to the following equation:

$$S_n = (S'_n) = \frac{360}{\sum_{1}^{B} (S'_n)}. \tag{8.10}$$

8.4.2. Use of porous materials for fan blades

The effect on fan noise of using a porous fan blade surface has been studied

TABLE 8.1. *Noise reduction of a model fan* when different porous materials were used (Tseo 1974)*

Porous material	Volume flow	dB(A)	Octave-band levels (dB)							
			62	125	250	500	1k	2k	4k	8k
No material	100%	60	Fan noise 54	59.5	54.5	52.5	50.5	58	50.5	37.5
				Noise reduction (dB)						
1/8 inch thick polyurethane foam, 2 lb/ft³	92%	2.0	0.5	2.5	2.5	0.0	0.0	2.5	0.5	0.0
1/8 inch thick polyurethane foam 12 lb/ft³	91%	2.0	0.0	3.5	0.0	−5.5	−2.0	8.0	2.5	−0.0
1/16 inch thick Fibreglass 3.5 lb/ft³, 4–10 μm fibre diameter.	94%	4.0	0.0	3.5	0.0	−3.0	0.0	7.5	3.0	2.0
0.012 inch thick metal fibre 0.070 lb/in³, 8 μm fibre diameter	95%	3.0	3.0	4.0	−1.5	−2.5	1.0	7.5	0.5	−1.5

* 3-blade axial fan with a diameter of 17.8 cm.

TABLE 8.2. *Comparison of sound pressure levels at same point in noise field for different fan–rotor couplings for a claw-rotor alternator (Yang 1977)*

Frequency (Hz)	Sound pressure level* at same point (dB)			
	N = 7000 (r/min)		N = 5834 (r/min)	
	rigid coupling	special coupling	rigid coupling	special coupling
6N	70	66	68	65
12N	70	66	73	69
13N	67	64	65	60
18N	76	73	66	66
36N	79	72	68	65

*1 per cent narrow-band sound pressure level. N = speed (r/min).

experimentally by a number of researchers. A reduction in sound level of 2 to 4 dBA was achieved (Tseo 1974) when the steel blade surface of a small axial fan was coated with a thin layer of porous material such as polyurethane, fibreglass or metal fibres (see Table 8.1). However, as also shown in Table 8.1, the fan flow rate was reduced by 5% to 9%. Chanaud (1972) reported that the use of porous fan blades made of fine fibres with 80% porosity, i.e. 20% dense, gave a sound level reduction of 5 to 10 dBA and a considerable reduction in flow rate for a 20.3 cm diameter fan, compared with solid fan blades. His results suggest that the most effective mounting area for the porous material is the outer surface of the fan blade.

8.4.3. Use of special fan–rotor coupling

Many variable speed electrical machines are equipped with cooling fans rigidly coupled to the rotor. The fan provides sufficient cooling air when the rotor speed is low but may give excessive cooling air and increased aerodynamic noise when the rotor is operating at high speeds. It would be beneficial to use a special fan–rotor coupling which can drive the fan at a speed independent of the rotor speed. Yang (1977) used a special fan–rotor coupling to drive a 13-blade fan for a 6-claw rotor and 36-slot stator and obtained the noise reduction results shown in Table 8.2.

References

BONE, J.C.H. and SCHWARZ, K.K. (1973). Large a.c. motors. *Proc. Instn elect. Engrs* **120**, 10R, 1111–32.
CHANAUD, R.C. (1972). Noise reduction in propeller fans using porous blades at free-flow conditions. *J. acoust. Soc. Am.* **51**, 15–18.
CREMER, L. (1950). Die Wissenschaftlichen Grundlagen der Raumakustik, Bd. III. *Wellentheoretische Raumakustik*. Verlag, Leipzig.

FRANCOISE, P. (1970). The generation of noise and the response of the structures in asynchronous motors, particularly as far as the flow is concerned. *Appl. Acoust.* **3**, 23–45.

KING, A.J. (1944). The reduction of noise from air-conditioning systems. *Engineering* **157**, 501–4.

MELLIN, R.C. and SOVRAN, G. (1970). Controlling the tonal characteristics of the aerodynamic noise generated by fan rotors. *Trans. ASME, J. Basic Engng* **92**, 143–54.

PLONER, B. (1976). Aerodynamic noise in medium-sized asynchronous motors. *Brown Boveri Rev.* **63**, 493–9.

—— and HERZ, F. (1969). New design measures to reduce siren tones caused by centrifugal fans in rotating machines. *Brown Boveri Rev.* **56**, 280–7.

RENTZSCH, H. (1961). Luftstronungsgerausche in elektrichen Maschinen. *Elektrotech. Z. ETZ A* **82**, 792–8.

SCHULZ, G. (1964). *Contribution to the practice of noise reduction in industrial plants.* Verlag stahleisen, M.B.H., Dusseldorf.

TALAAT, M.E. (1957). Calculation of windage-noise power level in large induction motors. *Trans. Am. Inst. electr. Engrs* **76**, 46–55.

TSEO, G.G. (1974). Noise reduction of a miniature fan by using blade treatment. *J. Sound & Vib.* **32**, 153–8.

YANG, S.J. (1977). Noise from claw-rotor alternators. *Proc. 2nd Br. Conf. Teaching of Vibration and Noise,* Sheffield, pp. 37–43.

ZELLER, W. (1950). *Technische Larmabwehr.* Verlag, Stuttgart.

Index